Praise for

Success in Education through Peace, Healing, and Hope

"Policymakers, in their zeal to raise test scores, often forget what is involved in educating whole people—people who will be caring and loving as well as competent. Karen Rusthoven has given us a moving account of dedicated teachers engaged in heroic action. I wish all kids were fortunate enough to have a school like Community of Peace Academy, and I hope policymakers will read this."

Dr. Nel Noddings, Teachers College, Columbia University

"*Success in Education through Peace, Healing, and Hope* is more than a wish-dream for the future of education. For a dozen years, Karen Rusthoven and her colleagues have been living into this vision at the Community of Peace Academy, a charter school in St. Paul, Minnesota, serving a population of K-12 students who are tragically underserved by our society. With a program that helps students become whole persons who can live creatively in community, the CPA model has much to offer at a time when both public education and this generation of young people are in great need of fresh hope. Here is a book that offers authentic hope, grounded in practical experience and guided by hard-won wisdom."

Parker J. Palmer, author of *Let Your Life Speak* and *A Hidden Wholeness*

"*Success in Education through Peace, Healing, and Hope* is a creative attempt to infuse the life and curricula of American public schools with deep and spiritually grounded values that are truly universal. Karen Rusthoven is a hopeful voice for humanizing education through American public schools."

Dr. Thomas Groome, Boston College

"An upbeat, encouraging and practical portrait of an inner city school that every educator and every school can learn from. Karen shows what it means to help youngsters develop not only strong academic skills, but also the kind of peace-maker skills our country—and world—desperately need."

Joe Nathan, Director, Center for School Change,
Humphrey Institute, University of Minnesota

A PROFOUND NEW VISION FOR OUR PUBLIC SCHOOLS

Success in Education through Peace, Healing, and Hope

Karen J. Rusthoven, Ed.D.

Founder of Community of Peace Academy

SYREN BOOK COMPANY

MINNEAPOLIS

Most Syren books are available at special quantity discounts for bulk purchases for sales promotions, premiums, fund-raising, and educational needs. For details, write

Syren Book Company
Special Sales Department
5120 Cedar Lake Road
Minneapolis, MN 55416

Published by
Syren Book Company
5120 Cedar Lake Road
Minneapolis, MN 55416

Printed in the United States of America on acid-free paper

ISBN-13: 978-0-929636-72-6
ISBN-10: 0-929636-72-4

LCCN 2006936089

Cover design by Kyle G. Hunter
Cover photo by Jesse Tejeda
Interior photos by Charissa Uemura
Interior text design by Wendy Holdman

To order additional copies of this book see the form
at the back of this book or go to www.itascabooks.com.

*For the students and staff of
Community of Peace Academy,
whose daily decisions and choices
make the vision a reality*

At this crucial moment, we have an opportunity to revision education as a communal enterprise from the foundations up—in our images of reality, in our modes of knowing, in our ways of teaching and learning. Such a revisioning would result in a deeply ethical education, an education that would help students develop the capacity for connectedness that is at the heart of an ethical life.

Such an education would root ethics in its true and only ground, in the spiritual insight that beyond the broken surface of our lives there is a "hidden wholeness" on which all life depends. In such an education, intellect and spirit would be one, teachers and learners and subjects would be in vital community with one another, and a world in need of healing would be well served. That finally is the reason why the spirituality of education deserves and demands our attention.

PARKER PALMER,
TO KNOW AS WE ARE KNOWN

Contents

Preface

*By definition, wholeness and fullness of life would be the outcome of a
morally good life; the reward of one who consistently makes life-giving
decisions and choices for self and others, of his or her own free will. This is
a lofty and illusive goal.*

—————

In 1966, I entered the field of public education hoping to make
a difference in the lives of the least advantaged, to educate them
for economic prosperity. Nearly thirty years later, I founded Community of Peace Academy, a chartered public school, still hoping
to make a difference in the lives of the least advantaged, but having
a very different outcome in mind. My desire to create this public
school grew out of thirty years' lived experience as a parent of two
African American sons and as an educator, having served in both
public and Catholic diverse urban schools.

As a result of these experiences, I had come to believe that the
educational process must lead to more than economic prosperity.
It must lead to wholeness and fullness of life for all. By definition,
wholeness and fullness of life would be the outcome of a morally
good life; the reward of one who consistently makes life-giving decisions and choices for self and others, of his or her own free will.
This is a lofty and illusive goal.

At the same time, it is a goal that has a "life and death" urgency
about it. When I was a young mother, I used to believe that I could

give my children the world on a silver platter. I thought that if I set a good example, took them to church every Sunday, sent them to good schools, and provided them with rich life experiences, they would become "well-educated, economically successful, and happy adults" in my own definition of those terms. As I have watched my sons become young men, and as I have watched my stepchildren and nieces and nephews grow into adulthood, it has become clear to me that each one will choose, of his or her own free will, the direction of his or her life. The power of the human will, the free will, cannot be ignored in the education equation. To educate the whole person means that we must recognize and accept the truth: that all of the education in the world is for naught unless the student chooses, freely, to accept the teaching.

It is not surprising that as our prevalent culture has become increasingly more promiscuous, young people have become increasingly tempted to make decisions and choices that may look good at the time, but that ultimately do not lead to wholeness or fullness of life. Those who consistently make immoral decisions and choices ultimately become wards of the state, if they live long enough. I have witnessed this in the lives of my own children and others who have become incarcerated or whose young lives have been lost. Realizing that even when we try very hard to provide moral guidance, young people may or may not choose to follow it, makes it even more urgent that as educators, we look for keys to the "free will" challenge.

It is my assumption that persons are more likely to make moral decisions if they are members of a moral community. If this is true, and if we care about our children, then we educators must dedicate ourselves to making every public school a moral learning community. The urban Catholic school provides a model for this.

In 1976, having taught in three public schools over a period of ten years, I was introduced to Catholic education, and for the first time, I became hopeful about the educational future of poor and powerless children in large urban areas. For the first time, I experienced schools that were making a difference in the lives of many of the urban children who traditionally do not succeed in public schools. I began to take note. As a non-Catholic "participant observer" in Catholic education for a period of sixteen years, it became apparent to me that much of what I was experiencing and observing was transferable to public education.

In 1991, the Minnesota legislature passed the first charter school law in the United States. Inspired by this new legislation and eager to create a public school founded upon principles borrowed from Catholic schools, I accepted an invitation to cofound a chartered public school. This new public school would be marketed to urban families whose options for school choice were often limited by their economic circumstances.

In 1995, Community of Peace Academy opened its doors on the east side of St. Paul, Minnesota, to 160 students in grades K to 5. This public school reform effort incorporates many features of urban Catholic education—features that have been proved to be effective in educating those children and youth who continue to fail, in alarmingly large numbers, in our nation's public schools. The profoundly moral vision of this public school is as follows:

Our desired outcome is to educate the whole person— mind, body and will—for peace, justice, freedom, compassion, wholeness and fullness of life for all.

Now in its twelfth year, Community of Peace Academy has grown to an enrollment of 600 students in grades K to 12. They are Hmong, African American, Eritrean, Hispanic, and European American. Eighty-three percent qualify for free and reduced-price meals, and nearly 70 percent are learning English as their second language. Twelve percent qualify for special education services. They mirror the diversity of most urban public school populations in America. By following this new vision, a diverse community of students, staff, and parents are finding at Community of Peace Academy, in addition to a quality academic program, wholeness and fullness of life for themselves and others.

Success in Education through Peace, Healing, and Hope explores this unorthodox approach in six distinct parts. The chapters in Part I discuss current ethical and moral challenges that face our public schools and present the case for a new vision. Part II offers a theoretical framework for education for fullness of life for all. It takes a serious look at Catholic schools and lessons that can be learned there. Part III introduces Community of Peace Academy as a model of this uncommon reform agenda in action, and explores some of the key elements that have assured adherence to the school's vision of wholeness and fullness of life for all. In 2001, I completed a qualitative research study titled *First Fruits: Adolescent Moral Development at Community of Peace Academy*. The study focused upon the students in the tenth grade who were in the fifth grade when the school opened in 1995, and included both interviews and narrative accounts, based upon participant observations. Schools are complex social systems, and education is a highly moral enterprise. These narratives are included in Parts IV and V both to capture this complexity and to illustrate the moral character of each incident or event.

We learn to be moral human beings, not so much by reading and studying about morality as by experiencing it in community. Morality is a choice we make. We humans are inspired to make moral decisions and choices based upon the quality of our relationships and the experiences we have had. The narratives in Part IV address the challenges faced in building caring, supportive, I–Thou relationships within a diverse urban school. Those in Part V illustrate the importance of experiences in building moral character in youth.

In nearly all cases, students' names have been changed in these narratives; the names of adults have not been changed. A narrative also appears in Chapter 3 of Part I. It is included to illuminate the discussion and is printed in italics. When students' letters or speeches are used, they are attributed to their authors. Quotations attributed to students or members of the staff are taken from the qualitative study as well. Tim McGowan joined the Community of Peace Academy staff in 1997 and taught seventh- and eighth-grade math and science until 2002, when he became the assistant principal at the high school. You will find him in various parts of the book in each of these roles.

Part VI, the book's conclusion, contains three chapters. Chapter 25, "Spiritual Warfare," recounts the events of an exceptionally challenging day in the life of Community of Peace Academy. Such days are not uncommon in public schools all across America. This chapter acknowledges the spiritual battle that is raging around us and illustrates how a public school, when focused upon wholeness and fullness of life for all, can sustain a culture of hope and joy even under the most dismal circumstances. Chapter 26, "Love in Action," makes a strong case for returning public education to parents and teachers. The closing chapter, "The Final Form of Love," acknowledges the magnitude of the challenge inherent in implementing this new vision for America's public schools. At the same time, it offers great hope that such a thing is possible through the power of forgiveness.

Acknowledgments

I wish to acknowledge the following people who, over the years, have made significant contributions to this work:

My parents, Ruth Jamison Bossart and William Bossart, who gave me my moral compass.

My husband, Jay, and my family for unconditional love and support.

My son Benjamin, whose struggles add wisdom and urgency to my work.

Sister Patricia DeMoully, who taught me what it means to be a servant-leader.

The people of Holy Name Catholic School for their faith in a non-Catholic principal.

Dr. Mary Katherine Hamilton, whose teaching helped to shape a new vision.

Dr. Mary Maher and Dr. Bob Brown, who encouraged me to keep going.

All who read my manuscript in various forms: Susan Rolfe, Molly Heisenfelt, Paula Sanchez, Steve Dickinson,

Catherine Guisan, Mary Maher, Bob Brown, and Bill Peter. Your comments and encouragement were invaluable.

The good people at Syren Book Company for a book we can all be proud of.

Introduction

As we come together to examine this new vision, we must be courageous in our thinking and creative in our imagining. We must be willing to ask hard questions and to grapple with the implications of honest answers.

This book is about a new vision for America's public schools. It is written for all Americans who are passionate about public education. Who are we passionate ones? We are liberals and conservatives, teachers and administrators, students and parents, young people and old people, union leaders and members of school boards, businesspeople, researchers, and members of state legislatures and the federal government. We represent all races and cultures and all religious groups. We are common people and people of influence. We Americans care passionately about our public schools, and for many of us, change comes hard.

Each of us has our own vision. If we attended public schools, or if we are public educators, our vision has been shaped by the time and place of our own experience. In America, one's economic status, race, and culture profoundly influence one's vision of public schools. If we are businesspeople, our vision will be shaped by the impact of public education upon the bottom line. Our vision of public education may also be profoundly affected by our political or religious persuasion.

Currently, our federal government has its own vision for America's public schools. The government has mandated that no child be left behind. By 2013, every child in the United States, regardless of race, culture, language, or disability, must, by law, be "proficient" on state-mandated tests. This vision was inspired by a desire to close the achievement gap that has persisted in America's public schools between students living in poverty and those who are economically advantaged. While the No Child Left Behind legislation is noble in its intent, our nation's children need and deserve even more from their public schools. Having experienced four decades of ineffective public education reform initiatives, and having witnessed the promise of a new vision, I can no longer remain silent.

As we come together to examine this new vision, we must be courageous in our thinking and creative in our imagining. We must be willing to ask hard questions and to grapple with the implications of honest answers. We do know what works. We have many examples of schools that are achieving success in educating all children, regardless of race, culture, or economic status.

Too often, the public school establishment dismisses the good work of such schools because they are not traditional public schools. The wisdom of these schools may also be overlooked by public education reformers because many who work in public schools have never visited such a school or are simply unaware that they exist. Much of what you will find here is borrowed from these schools.

Public school change of the magnitude I am recommending is historically driven by significant social unrest or a dramatic realization that the present system is failing. The No Child Left Behind legislation was driven by such factors and provides strong evidence that sweeping educational reform is needed. Never before has the federal government intervened so heavily into the education of our public school children, yet the NCLB vision is too limited to prepare our children for the world they and their descendants will inhabit.

Americans are a diverse people and becoming more diverse each year. We live in a world that has been made totally interdependent by the influence of technology and the realities of limited space and limited resources. If we hope to achieve and maintain peace, within our schools and within our nation and world, we must ensure that future citizens are both highly intelligent and highly moral human beings.

We need a vision that works for all, not just for some. The answer to our nation's educational woes lies in ensuring that each child attends a public school that is a safe, caring, moral learning community in which all members strive for moral goodness. Within such communities, life-giving relationships and experiences are nurtured, and there is potential for all to achieve whole and full lives.

Join me as we examine the awe-inspiring potential of educating America's public school children for peace, justice, freedom, compassion, wholeness, and fullness of life for all. My sincere hope for this book is that it will help usher in a new day for public education in our nation; that it will inspire and empower many within the public school community to embrace and implement this vision. It is a vision rooted in ancient wisdom and, if taken seriously and applied unwaveringly, has the power to transform not only our public schools but our very lives. That is, in fact, what education is meant to do.

PART I

Saved by Hope

Nothing that is worth doing can be achieved in our lifetime; therefore, we must be saved by hope.

REINHOLD NIEBUHR,
THE IRONY OF AMERICAN HISTORY

CHAPTER 1

In Search of Justice

All my life, for as long as I can remember, I had had a strong sense of racial justice. However, being Jamison and Benjamin's mother changed my worldview. I was a white woman looking at the world from the perspective of an African American mother. There was never a moment when I was not totally aware of the racial climate around me. This new awareness also strongly impacted the way in which I experienced my chosen profession.

When I was five years old, my family moved from St. Paul, Minnesota, to a small town on the Nebraska–Wyoming border. The main industry in this windswept town was sugar beets. Mexican migrants worked the fields. They would arrive in the backs of large rusty trucks—men, women, and children. My mother made it clear that this was not an acceptable way for people to have to live. It was my first awareness of social injustice.

I had just begun first grade when our family moved again, this time to a tiny town on the South Dakota prairie. Here I would attend grades one to five in a four-room wooden schoolhouse. There were outdoor toilets, and we were called to school by the ringing of a large bell that hung from the bell tower. It was in this town that I first encountered the Dakota Sioux. They lived near the railroad tracks in tents and were not well thought of by many people in town. Mother made it clear to us that we were never to talk badly of the Indians. Life was not easy for them.

It was in 1950, during my first-grade year in South Dakota, that wealthy relatives invited my mother, my two sisters, and me to visit them in Miami, Florida. They sent us tickets, and we rode the train all the way to Miami. As we traveled through the Deep South, I was introduced to the harsh realities of racial segregation. I realize now that my vivid memories of these things were enhanced as I witnessed my mother's reaction to them: separate drinking fountains, separate bathrooms, service provided by African Americans only, and the terrible chain gangs, all African American, who were forced to work along the tracks. I will never forget their eyes as they watched our train pass by.

My strong interest in other cultures mirrored my mother's interest. When I was ten years old, my family moved back to St. Paul, where eventually, I attended a racially and culturally diverse public high school on the west side. Friendships made during those years with Ukrainian, Lebanese, and Latino classmates have endured. I graduated from college in 1966, and, as was my goal, returned to my old west side neighborhood to teach third grade.

My students were predominantly Mexican American, as had been my high school classmates. From 1966 to 1970, I devoted myself to them. They were the focus of my life. I spent long hours planning my lessons and long days at school, where students often stayed after dismissal to help me with tasks such as cleaning chalkboards and erasers, decorating bulletin boards, feeding classroom pets, and watering plants. At 5:30 P.M. on one of those long days, my third-grade helper asked me if I had a job. When I explained to her that this was my job, she remarked incredulously, "You mean, you get paid for this!?" Such was my relationship with my students. I loved them, and I loved their parents. They were my neighbors, members of my community. I wanted the very best for them, and I gave them the best I had to offer. For many, it would not be enough.

When I began teaching on the west side of St. Paul in 1966, my students had the lowest test scores in the city. I soon became keenly aware of the injustices that existed in our public schools. College friends had accepted teaching positions in more affluent public school districts, and we compared notes. My students may have been public school students, but public did not mean equal. My students were the have-nots. Their parents were poor, and many spoke little, if any, English. They had no voice. They had no one to advocate for them. The quality of their education was severely jeopardized by their economic status. In my youthful idealism, I wrote a letter to the superintendent requesting adequate resources for my students. My principal was not pleased. In truth, the principal himself had very little power to change what was wrong with the system under which my students languished.

In 1970, after four years of marriage, my husband and I decided to adopt our first child. Minnesota had done pioneering work in interracial adoptions, and we told the agency that we would be happy to adopt a child of any race. After what seemed like an eternity, we received the call informing us that our son was African American and German. We named him Jamison in memory of my mother's father, my grandpa Jamison. Two years later, in October of 1972, we adopted our second son, Benjamin. This time, we had requested that our child be African American, and so he was.

Before adopting our sons, I could never have imagined the intense power of a mother's love. I had been a teacher for four years, and I truly loved my students. Yet, the first time I held Jamison in my arms, I knew that my life would never be the same again. I was overcome by the miracle that was this tiny child and the miracle that had brought him to us. My faith informed me that I was not holding this baby boy by chance. I was deeply grateful to God and to the woman who had given birth to him. Her unfathomable gift had allowed me to be a mother.

All my life, for as long as I can remember, I had had a strong sense of racial justice. However, being Jamison and Benjamin's mother changed my worldview. I was a white woman looking at the world from the perspective of an African American mother. There was never a moment when I was not totally aware of the racial climate around me. This new awareness also strongly impacted the way in which I experienced my chosen profession.

In 1976, when Jamison entered kindergarten, I enrolled him in the public school to which he was assigned on the west side of St. Paul, where we lived. At that time, I was teaching first grade at another public school in St. Paul. This was a magnet school and was part of our district's desegregation plan. It was supposedly one of the best schools in the district. The program was designed to attract the parents of white children, to entice them to consider allowing their children to attend school with African American children. The necessity of pleasing white parents turned the politics behind this school against African American children and their families. Once again they had no voice and no power.

Parents attracted to this magnet school were, for the most part, well-educated, professional people who were liberal in their thinking. Parents from the immediate neighborhood were, for the most part, poor, and many of them were not well educated. The children in this magnet school therefore came from two distinct worlds and had as little in common as did their parents. Yet, no attention was given to this disparity. Nothing was done to assist these children in bridging the cultural divide that separated them. Nothing was done to help them establish caring relationships with one another. African American students were soon overrepresented in remedial classes and behavior referrals.

As I experienced this, I realized that I was watching from an entirely new perspective. Now the injustices I witnessed became deeply personal. This was not about justice for someone else's children, it was about justice for *my* children. The pain was real. I would not allow the system to treat my children in this way. I would protect my sons from this kind of environment. And then came the profound realization that, in truth, if it was not good enough for my children, it was not good enough for anyone's children.

America's public schools are not equal. There are vast differences in the public school education that children of the wealthy and children of the poor receive. Districts in wealthy suburbs and in poor urban areas are often every bit as unequal today as were the schools of the South before the Supreme Court's historic ruling in *Brown v. Board of Education* outlawed segregation in our nation's public schools in 1954. Even magnet schools, created to integrate public schools, most often do not provide equal education for all students within their walls.

If we truly care about the education of the children in America's public schools, it is morally unconscionable to continue to support the status quo. It is equally unacceptable to place blame for the persistent achievement gap upon the often powerless and voiceless teachers who work on the front lines every day in a system that is broken. We must set aside our politics and open our minds and hearts to a new vision for public school students and for those who teach them.

Too many people who work in public education, and who have power and voice regarding public schools, would not and do not send their own children to the schools they oversee. We who are passionate about public education must challenge ourselves at a deeply moral level. Whether we are administrators, union leaders, members of school boards, teachers, members of the state or federal government, businesspeople, parents, or concerned residents without children, if the public education we provide would not be good enough for our own children, it is not good enough.

CHAPTER 2

Expanding Our Vision

If our graduates are not able to find whole and full lives for themselves, the years spent in our institutions have surely not served them well. From an instrumental perspective, each young person who is not able to find his or her rightful place in society is an invaluable resource lost to our nation. From a moral perspective, a human life is a terrible thing to waste.

Under our present system of compulsory education, in order to graduate, students attend school until the age of eighteen. What is our desired outcome for America's public school graduates? What are our hopes and dreams for these, our sons and daughters? What vision drives our current system of public education?

I was raised in a family that believed the purpose of education was to prepare us to leave home, to enter the world of work. I remember my mother telling us that when she and her sister and brothers turned eighteen, their father made it clear that they needed to be on their own. They were expected to get a job or, in the case of Mother and her sister, get married and leave home, and they did.

When my sister reached the age of eighteen, she married her high school sweetheart and left home. When I was eighteen, I chose to go to college. I was the first member of my family to do so, and my parents gladly extended my welcome for another four years. I married immediately upon graduation from college, and my husband and I moved into our own apartment. My younger sister did the same. We all followed the pattern that Grandpa Jamison had set for our family.

Times have changed. Eighteen-year-olds no longer can expect to get a job that will support them, much less one that will allow them to support a family. Today, even college graduates often live with their parents until they can get their economic feet on the ground. It is increasingly more challenging for our young people to find independence, to launch themselves into the mainstream of American life. For those with special needs, the challenges can appear overwhelming.

When our sons were young, I often dressed them alike. I made every effort to ensure that whatever was given to one, was equally given to the other. The boys could not have been more different. Jamison loved cars and trucks and all kinds of sports and adventure. For the most part, he listened to me and took discipline to heart. He had a strong sense of cause and effect and learned from his mistakes. Benjamin loved music, table games, video games, and drama. He was impulsive. As my mother used to say, "If you don't want Benjamin to touch something, move it." It soon became apparent that no matter how I tried, I could not keep everything equal.

As Benjamin approached adolescence, it became evident that he had many emotional needs that were interfering significantly with his development. He struggled with adoption issues and with his own sexual identity. He was diagnosed with a learning disability. In spite of all our efforts on his behalf, things did not go well for Benjamin. It became necessary for him to spend his sophomore year in a residential treatment center. Through my work as a Catholic school principal and the personal heartache of Benjamin's experience, my philosophy of education began to change.

Watching our son's struggles made me keenly aware that our desired outcome for graduates needed to focus not only on their *on caring* [handwritten marginal note]

minds and bodies but also on their spirits or wills. It was not what we wanted for our eighteen-year-old children that would determine the outcome of their lives. It was rather what our eighteen-year-old children wanted for themselves that would shape their destinies. If, by the time they graduated from high school, our daughters and sons were not, *of their own free will*, making decisions and choices that would lead to mental, emotional, physical, and spiritual health and well-being for themselves, their futures would be in jeopardy. Moreover, unless they were making similar decisions and choices on behalf of others, their presence in the world might jeopardize the futures of those around them.

Realizing how sincerely my husband and I had tried to assist Benjamin in his development, and witnessing the pain of his inability, as a young man, to find his place in society and to support himself, I gained a new and profound respect for the challenge that we educators face. If our graduates are not able to find whole and full lives for themselves, the years spent in our institutions have surely not served them well. From an instrumental perspective, each young person who is not able to find his or her rightful place in society is an invaluable resource lost to our nation. From a moral perspective, a human life is a terrible thing to waste.

The No Child Left Behind Act of 2002, our nation's most recent vision for our public school students, was written to ensure that every child, regardless of culture, race, economic status, or disability would achieve a predetermined level of academic success by 2013, thus eradicating the long-standing achievement gap. In spite of good intentions, No Child Left Behind is another tremendously costly and disruptive reform agenda that is destined to fail the very students it was designed to assist. Like so many reform agendas before it, its focus is too narrow and does not address the heart of the matter: students come to us whole; they have free will; they are not widgets and will not be manipulated.

Most students on the wrong side of the achievement gap live in poverty. The problems that plague their lives are not only academic in nature. Their physical, emotional, and spiritual challenges are often enormous—so enormous that, on any given day, they may overshadow academic needs. I am in no way suggesting that the situation for these students is hopeless. Quite the contrary, I have tremendous hope for their lives.

In our public schools, these children can reach not only their full academic potential but also their full potential physically, emotionally, and spiritually. They can be empowered and inspired, in public schools, to make life-giving decisions and choices of their own free will, not only for themselves, but for others as well.

Such an outcome will not be achieved in a system of public education that focuses all of its attention and resources on academic outcomes. Those of us who have accepted a role in the education of America's public school children have accepted the highest moral mandate a nation can bestow. We must approach our work with the highest possible level of integrity. Our children's lives and the future of our nation depend upon our getting it right. We must expand our vision. Eighteen comes soon. There is no time to waste.

— CHAPTER 3 —

Overcoming the Effects of Poverty

Bracey's findings regarding the effects of poverty on academic achievement come as no surprise to those who labor on the front lines in public schools that serve the poor. What is most enlightening, is his acknowledgment of the fact that, in spite of their best efforts, precious few schools have found a way to overcome the effects of poverty and even fewer have been able to *sustain* the effort required to overcome the debilitating effects of poverty over time.

~

Vua Vang steps into my office. "Are you busy?" I invite her in and ask what's on her mind. She explains that she's concerned about the attitude of some of her fourth-grade students toward the school rules. They've been trying to have a discussion about the rules in morning meeting, and some of the kids are saying that their mothers have told them that if anyone fights you, you should fight back. She wonders if I would join their Morning Meeting tomorrow. I tell her that I would be delighted.

As I enter the room the next morning, the children are bringing their chairs to the circle for morning meeting. They make a place for me. We go around the circle and each one is greeted. Ms. Vang then reminds them why I am here. The children have prepared questions for me to answer. I glance through their papers. They are earnest, sometimes angry questions.

One child asks: "What if someone started hitting on you for nothing what are you supposed to do? My mom said to hit them back. You said tell on them if they keep hitting you. If my mom finds out that I didn't hit them back I'll be in trouble."

The children are watching me with great expectation. I notice three African American girls who look at me with detached, somewhat defiant expressions. They are new students unfamiliar to me.

I explain that Community of Peace Academy is a very different kind of school and that people who choose it are agreeing to be peace builders. They are agreeing to solve problems with their heads and with their hearts, not with their fists. I tell them that there are nearly fifty other public schools in St. Paul and many other charter schools and private schools to choose from. No one has to choose Community of Peace Academy, but those who do choose it, agree to practice nonviolence.

I read the next question—"What if your mom told you to hit them back, but you don't so you go and tell someone but they keep trying to fight you, what do you do?"—and begin to process it with the students:

"What do we call this kind of behavior? There is a name for it."

"Threatening."

"Yes, but what other word could we use?" I wait for a response and then answer myself: "The word is 'bullying.' A person who keeps trying to fight you is a bully. What do you need to do if someone won't leave you alone?"

"Seek a wise person."

"Yes! You need to tell someone. It is never OK for anyone to threaten you or to fight you. If you don't seek a wise person, then the bully wins. Even adults need to seek a wise person sometimes."

We take their questions one at a time. As we make our way down the list, the expressions on faces soften and become more childlike. The vulnerability of these children is painfully apparent:

"If somebody brings guns and knives and they don't tell you, what can you do?"

"Some people used to threaten me. I tell the teacher then the next day they threaten me again. What would I do?"

"What if a kid starts to hit you and you can't find a wise person?"

"What if somebody brings real guns and knives? What will we do?"

I field each question as honestly as I can. I try not to minimize their concerns. They are all too real. I explain that peace building is not easy. It takes great courage. It doesn't mean that you let people mistreat you or take advantage of you. It means that you learn to use your head and your heart to resolve trouble. You need to avoid dangerous people and places if you can, and you need help if you are being bullied or threatened. That is what wise people are for. Go to an adult that you trust and ask for help. If they don't listen, go to another wise person until someone listens.

Most of the children seem more at peace. Freddie, however, can't stop asking questions: "But what if the person is bigger and they are really strong? What if they are around you all the time? What if there isn't a wise person to ask?"

We run out of time and the others leave for the gym. I put my arm around his shoulder and we talk.

"Is someone bullying you, Freddie?"

"Yes."

"Who is it?"

"My brother Jerome. He does it all the time and I tell my mom but she can't do anything." I know this family and I know Jerome to be an emotionally disturbed child. I tell Freddie that I will call his mom.

I catch her at work. She puts me on hold, then excuses herself and calls back a few minutes later. I explain my conversation with Freddie, and she unburdens herself. Everything he told me is true. Jerome is thirteen. He bullies her, too. Jerome is currently in detention. He has been convicted of five major assaults. His court date is in October, and she fears that they will send him home again. She has had people with guns driving and walking by her house because Jerome has assaulted their son or brother. She has tried everything. No one will help. She sent Jerome to live with his father, but after three weeks his father sent him back. She pleaded with him to keep him but he wouldn't. She fears her family will be the next family that they find dead.

She has a fifteen-year-old son who also is in constant trouble. The two older boys are completely out of control. Her present husband moved out because he couldn't take the constant turmoil. She is now alone with the two older boys, Freddie, his sister, who is in first grade at Community of Peace Academy, and her infant daughter. She is desperate. She lets the three younger children sleep with her to protect them from their brothers, but she can't always be there because she has to work.

I tell her that I will see if I can find any resources for her. She thanks me for listening. I call an intake worker at Ramsey County Child Protection and get a recording. The worker will be back early the following week. Since Jerome is in detention until October, I leave a message and ask the intake worker to call me when she returns. Sometimes we seek a wise person and we have to wait our turn.

Growing up has always been a journey fraught with moral dilemmas for young people of all cultures, races, and economic states. Adolescents are challenged to decide for or against such things as cheating on tests, truanting, smoking, using alcohol, taking drugs, having sex, and shoplifting. Even decisions regarding choice of peer group, music, movies, and video games are moral in nature. In my youth, these moral challenges were offset by the values of my family, my church, and my community. In addition to these positive influences, the prevailing American culture most often encouraged moral behaviors. Most movies, music, and TV programs sent the same moral messages, as did the real people in my life.

Today, the prevailing youth culture does not encourage fullness of life for all. It does not encourage young people to make decisions and choices that lead to mental, physical, emotional, and spiritual health for themselves and others. Most music, advertising, movies, video games, and TV programming aimed at young audiences promote materialism, self-satisfaction, promiscuous sex, drugs, and violence. Driven by an in-your-face attitude of anger and alienation from adults, the words of many songs aimed at adolescents are hammered out, pounding morality into oblivion. The Internet pours fuel on the fire by offering ready access to pornography and a complete array of morally bereft Web sites. Young people of all races, cultures, and economic states are vulnerable.

For youth living in poverty, all of these negative influences are magnified. Whether negative moral influences cause poverty, or poverty exacerbates negative moral influences, is a debate for another day. It is surely true that there is a strong correlation between them. Unemployment and underemployment breed despair. Despair fosters crime, the abuse of alcohol and drugs, and irresponsible sexual activity. Parents living in poverty often fall prey to this vicious circle. Others struggle, against powerful odds, to raise their children without the support of a partner. Still others work two and three jobs to make ends meet and are seldom at home to monitor their children's activities. Parents who do not speak English may not understand the powerful negative influences of the music, TV, Internet, and video media to which their children are exposed. Even when immigrant parents try to offer guidance, their children may dismiss their wisdom because it seems not to apply to American culture.

Schools in major urban areas, as well as schools in many remote communities, serve large numbers of children who live in poverty. These children do not leave the realities of their daily lives at the schoolhouse door. As the narrative at the beginning of this chapter illustrates, they bring them with them each day as they enter their classrooms. Many are angry. They do not believe in bright futures where they will have access to the lives they see others living on television and in the movies. Some have never known a family member who worked for a living. They have no vision of a bright tomorrow and little hope that they might personally get there.

Too often, the children of the poor live in fear and mistrust. They fear all who are different from them. They fear those who are stronger and meaner and more powerful. Frequently, they have developed a "dog eat dog" mentality. They make fun of others to give themselves some sense of control over their lives. They stick with their own kind and defend their own and their territory at all costs. The gangs and gang activity that result from this mentality often approach the level of warfare. Many who work in urban schools, myself included, have attended the funerals of children whose lives were cut short by gang violence. Violent acts have occurred in recent years in public schools across the country and seem to be perpetrated by children from all cultures, races and economic states. What was unthinkable in the past has become all too common today.

Every three years since 1989, the voluntary Minnesota Student Survey (MSS) has been administered to more than 100,000 public school students in grades 6, 9, and 12 across the state. The survey, which is endorsed by the Minnesota Departments of Education, Health, Human Services, Public Safety, and Corrections, addresses relevant issues that confront youth. Results of the survey mirror national trends.

According to the Minnesota Department of Health (2003), alarming disparities exist between communities of color and the white community in several areas of health and well-being. Consistently since 1995, MSS results report more children of color engaging in such behaviors as smoking, sexual activity, carrying weapons, and fighting than their white counterparts.

African American, Asian, Latino, and American Indian youth consistently report experiencing emotional distress more frequently than do white youth. According to 2001 MSS results, these young people were, on average, nearly twice as likely to report feelings of discouragement and hopelessness as their white counterparts. These results held true for all grade levels. Students were considered as having high emotional distress if they reported experiencing two or more of the following four conditions:

+ Felt stress or pressure "almost more than I can take."

+ Felt sad "all the time" or "most of the time."

+ Felt discouraged or hopeless, "extremely so" or "quite a bit."

 ✦ Felt nervous, worried or upset "all the time" or "most of
 the time."

Among students who exhibited all four types of distress, 40.5 percent reported an attempted suicide in the past year, compared to
only 2.4 percent of those exhibiting none of the four types of distress (MDH, 2004). Among students who attempt suicide, 58 percent reported feelings of hopelessness as compared to only 7 percent
of students who have no thoughts of suicide. Between 1998 and
2002, suicide was the third leading cause of death for 10- to 14-
year-olds (30 deaths) in Minnesota and the second leading cause of
death for 15- to 19-year-olds (170 deaths). Among adolescents and
young adults, suicide rates were three times higher in the American
Indian community than in other racial/ethnic group.

On March 22, 2005, *St. Paul Pioneer Press* headlines screamed:
Deadly day at school. TOLL: Red Lake teen kills 9 and himself,
wounds at least 12. SUSPECT: Sophomore had foreshadowed
shootings online. IMPACT: Deadliest school shooting in U.S.
since Columbine. Floyd Jourdain Jr., chairman of the Red Lake
Band of Chippewa, called it, "without a doubt, the darkest hour
in the history of our tribe." We ignore the impact of poverty upon
the lives of America's children to our nation's peril.

The impact of poverty upon the academic performance of our
nation's children cannot be ignored. Each time test scores of public school students are published, the demographics of each school
are noted. Most often, as the free and reduced-price lunch count
goes up, the test scores go down. In fact, most often, there is a near
perfect relationship between these factors: if the free and reduced-
price lunch count is 10 percent higher in a given school, the test
scores will be almost exactly 10 percent lower.

The nationally known policy analyst, researcher, and author Gerald
Bracey shared the findings of his research regarding the education of poor children in the United States at the 2002 Minnesota

Education Summit held in St. Paul. To determine the effect of poverty on academic achievement, Bracey analyzed test scores of children in 8,761 California schools. He found that of schools with 75 percent poverty, 9 were among the top 25 percent of the 8,761 schools on state tests the first year of his study, and only 5 remained in the top 25 percent the second year. Of schools with 90 percent poverty, 3 of the 8,761 were in the top 25 percent for one year, and none remained in the top 25 percent for a second year.

Bracey concluded that, as a nation, we already know where we need to target our efforts—namely, on effectively educating poor children—and that we do not need to test every child in every grade every year. He noted that critics like to state that we shouldn't use poverty as an excuse, but that the facts of his research and the research of many others cannot be ignored. He also pointed out that in every country of the world, there is a similar correlation between poverty and achievement.

Bracey's findings regarding the effects of poverty on academic achievement come as no surprise to those who labor on the front lines in public schools that serve the poor. What is most enlightening is his acknowledgment of the fact that, in spite of their best efforts, precious few schools have found a way to overcome the effects of poverty, and even fewer have been able to *sustain* the effort required to overcome the debilitating effects of poverty over time.

In his research, Bracey acknowledged that staff members in high-poverty schools with high test scores devote hundreds of hours of extra work to helping their students achieve. About six years ago I heard a presentation by Yvonne Chan, principal of Vaughn Next Century Learning Center in the Los Angeles Unified School District. Vaughn was a large, impoverished, decrepit, and failing traditional public school that was converted to a charter school and became a blue ribbon school with excellent test scores in a period of a few short years. At the conclusion of her inspirational presentation, I asked Ms. Chan privately why it is that when we know what works, so few schools are doing it. She looked me squarely in the eye and said with a resigned tone, "Because it is so much work."

In 2004, the Office of Innovation and Improvement in the U.S. Department of Education published a book titled *Successful Charter Schools*. Following a national search of nearly three thousand charter schools, the authors chose eight to highlight in this publication; Community of Peace Academy was among them. As I reflected upon the information contained in this book, I was struck by the high level of commitment, hard work, and dedication of the people who worked in the eight schools. For those working in areas of high poverty, their efforts were, in some cases, nearly superhuman. The inability to sustain such a superhuman effort *over time* has sabotaged the long-term success of many reform initiatives.

In June of 2006, the Office of Innovation and Improvement invited the principals of the eight charter schools featured in *Successful Charter Schools* to serve on an advisory committee regarding the publication of a new book featuring K–8 charter schools that are effectively closing the achievement gap. It turned out that only three of the original eight principals remained at their schools.

Just as the key to our students' long-term success lies in inspiring and empowering them to choose wholeness and fullness of life for themselves and others, so the key to long-term success for educators, especially those working in high-poverty schools, lies in inspiring and empowering them to find wholeness and fullness of life, not only for their students, but also for themselves. Only under such conditions can public educators hope to sustain the effort required to overcome the effects of poverty.

Teachers and students benefit equally from their participation in schools that are guided by a clear ethical and moral vision. Both teachers and students thrive when their spirits are nurtured, when they are treated with kindness, given support, and appreciated.

If our nation is serious about leaving no child behind, if we are sincere in our goal that every child in America will be academically proficient by 2013, then we must be about the business of educating our children and youth for wholeness and fullness of life for all. This goal will require that every public school is a moral learning community in which unconditional positive regard is extended to all: students, parents and members of the staff.

The powerful negative effects of poverty upon the lives of our citizens and their children are evident. The need for moral and spiritual guidance in the lives of our nation's public school children cannot be ignored. These precious children must not be left behind. Ensuring that they reach their full potential in our public schools will require a radically different approach to public education.

CHAPTER 4

Where Hope Comes From

Public school educators must begin to acknowledge that our children are more than physical and mental beings. They are also spiritual beings, and their spirits are fragile. The realities of their lives leave too many children with wounded spirits. When their spirits are crushed, they are as damaged as when their minds or bodies have been injured. Unless we first acknowledge and address the spiritual brokenness in the lives of these students, academic proficiency will remain a distant dream.

———

Last year I went through a lot. I got involved with a bad crowd. I was on drugs . . . I was on so many bad drugs. And I was skipping school. I came to school all pale, and the teachers, you all were really concerned about me. You knew something was wrong so you contacted my mom and you helped me through everything. You helped me turn my life around, and you did help get me off the drugs, because you guys sent me to a chemical assessment and then, I stopped.

And the teachers also helped me, because in my schoolwork, I wasn't doing so good. I dropped down a grade. And the teachers were really supportive. They helped me get back on track. They knew something was wrong and they helped me.

Community of Peace Academy, it just really helped me, the environment just totally changed me. Because, I was out of the environment for awhile, and my . . . my soul . . . it felt so different, because peace wasn't in me. I felt that I didn't belong for awhile, but when I came back, I knew that I did belong, and that everyone did care a lot about me . . . so I changed.

—*Community of Peace Academy Student*

Community of Peace Academy, a public charter school, was founded in response to the violence and brokenness of our times. It was founded upon the premise that we need to create public school communities where peace can be taught and practiced daily with great intentionality; schools in which our children can find hope and healing for their broken spirits.

The times in which we live are referred to as postmodern. We are told that old moral codes no longer apply. This is the age of relativism: we are living in a diverse society and when it comes to moral values, we can no longer assume that one size fits all.

It has been my experience that drugs and alcohol have the same negative impact on all human bodies. Sexually transmitted diseases do equal harm to all kinds of people. Children, all children, benefit equally from having parents who want and love them and can support them economically. Guns and knives injure all of us the same. Moral concepts such as honesty, respect, love, hope, justice, loyalty, and peace equally benefit human beings of all races and cultures today, as in the past, and their absence causes equal suffering to all, just as it always has.

At a recent meeting offered to assist service providers in interpreting the results of the Minnesota Student Survey, a participant stood and introduced herself as someone who had been involved in youth mental health services for more than twenty years. She said, "We have a choice of creating an environment in which healthy children can grow, or of treating their negative behaviors. We need to focus on the protective factors. Will we, as a community, focus upon developing our children in a healthy manner from inside out, or will we simply teach adults how to recognize suicidal behaviors in children? These are two very different things."

Her point was well taken. Such state and national surveys

identify the brokenness and are used to create programs to address the brokenness in the lives of our nation's children. In truth, we could be doing much to prevent the brokenness. We need both prevention and cure side by side all the time. Our public schools have the potential to do effective prevention; to be places in which healthy children can grow, from the inside out.

Public school educators must begin to acknowledge that our children are more than physical and mental beings. They are also spiritual beings, and their spirits are fragile. The realities of their lives leave too many children with wounded spirits. When their spirits are crushed, they are as damaged as when their minds or bodies have been injured. Unless we first acknowledge and address the spiritual brokenness in the lives of these students, academic proficiency will remain a distant dream.

Addressing the spiritual needs of children within public schools in the United States is uncharted territory. It is assumed that "seeking spiritual wholeness" and "public education" are mutually exclusive endeavors. This need not be the case.

Among the intentions of the First Amendment to the U.S. Constitution was the protection of our citizens from the imposition of a state religion and to ensure that each citizen's right to choose be protected. Traditionally, American children have been assigned to public schools. In this way, parents, particularly poor parents, have been denied freedom of choice regarding the education of their children.

If our nation were to turn its attention to providing all parents the right to choose their children's schools, the question of the separation of church and state, as it is applied to public education, would become irrelevant.

Finding a solution to the persistent emphasis on the separation of church and state within our public schools would prove a great benefit to public education for a number of reasons. In our attempts to honor the beliefs of all those assigned to our public schools, we have, at best, promoted concepts such as character education and multiculturalism, and at worst, promoted nothing in particular, leaving our students morally adrift.

One of the greatest strengths of our nation's private and parochial schools is their ability to state what they believe in and what they stand for at a deeply moral level, and to expect that all who choose to become members of the school community uphold its founding principles. Surprisingly, the freedom exercised by these schools in this regard has not threatened our democracy. On the contrary, private schools with a strong religious and/or moral focus have consistently produced excellent citizens. Throughout our nation's history, many of our most prominent leaders have been products of such schools, and many of our most prominent citizens choose these schools for their own children.

If we want all of America's schools to be excellent, then each school must be given the autonomy to determine its particular vision and mission. Moreover, in a great nation that prides itself on the freedoms its citizens enjoy, every parent must be given the freedom to choose the school his or her child will attend. The charter school movement is a step in the right direction. The fact that the children of the poor are overrepresented in charter schools is evidence that all parents and guardians, when given the freedom to do so, will eagerly choose what they believe to be the best schools for their children.

Having worked in Catholic schools for sixteen years, and having experienced the healing power of the inclusion of faith in the education process, I hope for a day when all families who wish for this may have it for their children. In the meantime, there is much more that all public schools could do to nurture the spiritual lives of their students and of the members of their staffs, without reference to a particular religion.

Public schools must strive to be kinder and gentler environments. In his book *Care of the Soul*, Thomas Moore (1992) discusses the importance of environment to the health of the human spirit. Children ought to feel at home in school. They deserve buildings and classrooms that are in good repair, clean, attractively painted, and attractively furnished. All living things benefit from natural light, and children are no exception. Schools need windows! They should be places where live plants and live children thrive together.

The human spirit derives comfort from looking upon beautiful things. Our public schools should be filled with artwork representative of the cultures of our students. Children should see beautiful representations of their culture, and the cultures of their classmates, everywhere. In addition, they should see their own beautiful work everywhere.

Too often, the arts are excluded from the lives of our public school children. This is more apt to be the case in schools in impoverished communities than in schools in wealthy neighborhoods. Art and music have the power to repair our brokenness. They give voice to our deepest thoughts and feelings. All public school children deserve access to this healing fountain. Quality arts education should most definitely be a funded federal mandate for children living in poverty.

Next to being loved, perhaps the most powerful force in mending the broken human spirit is giving love to others. Being of service to another human being, and feeling that person's sincere gratitude, affirms our most positive qualities. Every human being needs to be affirmed in this way. Experiences of service have the potential to change our students' lives for the better. For children living in poverty, service-learning is often transformational. Working on a Habitat for Humanity site or serving food to the homeless may awaken, for the first time, the realization that each student has the power not only to improve his or her own life but to make life better for someone else.

All children deserve to be affirmed and recognized by their classmates and teachers every day. Time intentionally set aside for these important community-building activities is essential to the well-being of students. In the process, trusting relationships are established that empower children to actively seek the emotional support they need, and their hearts are opened to receive it.

When students do not make life-giving decisions and choices, when rules are ignored or willfully violated, wise people must be there to patiently redirect them. These are opportunities for reflection and moral growth. This important work takes time and must be a priority in the education of the human will for moral goodness. Life-changing miracles often occur in the moral lives of students when a school's approach to discipline is restorative rather than punitive.

Schools cannot do the important work of educating for "fullness of life" alone; such a desired outcome absolutely requires that parents be equal partners. Home visits are an excellent way to build solidarity with parents. To ensure effective communication with all parents, public schools must employ some staff members who speak the same language as the parents of their students. Print material must be translated, and meetings must be interpreted. Parents without transportation must be transported. Child care must be provided for students' younger siblings.

Most important, public schools would do well to practice the principle of unconditional positive regard for all. Each member of the school community must be accepted and respected without exception. This approach, above all, mends the broken places in our lives and restores peace to the human soul.

Our nation's children need more from their public schools than they are getting. We must courageously broaden the desired outcomes for our public school children to a vision of wholeness and fullness of life for all. This expansion will demand the highest possible level of integrity on the part of all public educators. It will require that we tend to our own spiritual wholeness, each according to his or her own conscience, acknowledge the spiritual center of each of our students, and very intentionally structure our public schools and programs so as to nurture and care for their spirits. Against such, there is no law.

As was poignantly stated by the Community of Peace Academy student quoted at the beginning of this chapter, "I was out of the environment for awhile, and . . . my soul . . . felt so different, because peace wasn't in me. I felt that I didn't belong for awhile, but when I came back, I knew that I did belong, and that everyone did care a lot about me, so I changed."

We can no longer plead the First Amendment and use the postmodern excuse that morality is relative to absolve ourselves of responsibility for the moral lives of our students. By acknowledging and addressing students' social, emotional, and spiritual needs, we restore hope to their lives. If we are sincere in our efforts to close the achievement gap, public schools that serve large numbers of children living in poverty must make these things a priority.

PART II

Saved by Faith

—✦—

Nothing which is true or beautiful or good makes complete sense in any immediate context of history; therefore, we must be saved by faith.

REINHOLD NIEBUHR,
THE IRONY OF AMERICAN HISTORY

CHAPTER 5

Asking the Right Questions

In spite of a series of costly reforms over the past forty years, too many minority children still are not being well served by our nation's urban public schools. Is it possible that we have made a serious error in our diagnosis of the causes for their lack of success? Is it possible that we have been treating the wrong disease for the past forty years? Could that be the reason the patient has not been cured, in spite of our investment of billions upon billions of dollars and wave upon wave of reform initiatives? Could it be that the cure would require not an investment of financial resources but rather an investment of moral resources? These are questions worthy of our attention.

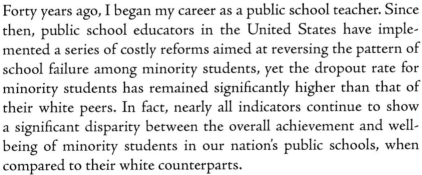

Forty years ago, I began my career as a public school teacher. Since then, public school educators in the United States have implemented a series of costly reforms aimed at reversing the pattern of school failure among minority students, yet the dropout rate for minority students has remained significantly higher than that of their white peers. In fact, nearly all indicators continue to show a significant disparity between the overall achievement and well-being of minority students in our nation's public schools, when compared to their white counterparts.

How is our nation addressing these ongoing disparities? A special edition of *Education Week* (January 11, 1999), titled, "Quality Counts: Rewarding Results, Punishing Failures," was devoted to current educational reform efforts and included such topics as raising standards, increased testing, more accountability, and increased sanctions.

In 2001, No Child Left Behind, the federal government's plan to reform our nation's public schools, was passed in Congress with bipartisan support. This unprecedented legislation joined record new funding to testing, accountability, and high standards so as to ensure educational excellence for every child.

In January 2005, the federal government extended the reach of No Child Left Behind to include our nation's high schools. The new High School Initiative provided $1.5 billion in the Fiscal Year 2006 budget; of that amount, $1.2 billion was intended for high school interventions to help states hold high schools accountable for teaching all students, and to provide effective interventions for those students not learning at grade level. The remaining $250 million was earmarked to fund required state assessments in high schools, to assure that high school diplomas are truly meaningful.

In spite of a series of costly reforms over the past forty years, too many minority children still are not being well served by our nation's urban public schools. Is it possible that we have made a serious error in our diagnosis of the causes for their lack of success? Is it possible that we have been treating the wrong disease for the past forty years? Could that be the reason the patient has not been cured, in spite of our investment of billions upon billions of dollars and wave upon wave of reform initiatives? Could it be that the cure would require not an investment of financial resources but rather an investment of moral resources? These are questions worthy of our attention.

Twenty years after I began my first teaching assignment, James Cummins (1986) published a study in which he suggested that a major reason attempts at educational reform had been unsuccessful since 1966, in empowering minority students, was that the relationships between teachers and students and between schools and minority communities had remained essentially unchanged over that twenty-year period. The same is true today. Cummins suggested that students' success in school was dependent upon the position their racial or cultural group held within the prevailing social order. He found that students from the same racial or ethnic group performed well in school in countries where their people group was esteemed and performed poorly in school in countries where their people group was not esteemed.

Cummins's findings mirror my own experience. During my forty years as teacher and principal in traditional public, parochial, and chartered public schools, I have observed that children, all children, perform well in schools that esteem and include their parents and are less likely to reach their full potential in schools where their parents are disregarded and ignored.

Cummins suggested that implementation of educational reform is dependent upon the extent to which educators, both collectively and individually, redefine their roles with respect to minority students and communities. Human relationships are the key to true reform. Public educators would do well to make note of this.

Under the current federal No Child Left Behind legislation, sanctions can be applied to schools in which the scores of all students do not reach a predetermined proficiency level on state-mandated tests. Ultimately, these schools may be taken over and reconstituted by the state. We must be wary of seeking our children's academic success to save our schools from sanctions. Such a system turns our precious children into "things" to be manipulated for our own gain. Desiring each student's wholeness and fullness of life, out of love for them, and making this our goal for 2013, would provide true hope that no one would be left behind in America's public schools. For years, Catholic schools have focused on such an outcome with great success.

In 1980, a major longitudinal research study was sponsored

by the National Center for Educational Statistics of the U.S. Department of Education. Titled *High School and Beyond*, this study directly concerned Catholic schools.

John Convey (1992) reported that an important finding from *High School and Beyond*, as well as from other studies, is that the achievement differences between Catholic schools and public schools are greatest for disadvantaged students, specifically, for those who are members of a racial or ethnic minority. Furthermore, Catholic schools were proved to be more successful than public schools in reducing the within-school differences between the academic achievement of minority students and that of other students. In short, the research showed that Catholic schools are particularly effective for disadvantaged students.

Among the findings Convey highlighted were the following:

1. The achievement advantage of Catholic schools over public schools generally was greatest for students whose parents had the lowest levels of education and the lowest incomes (Coleman et al., 1982; Greeley, 1982; Lee and Bryk, 1988, 1989;Lee and Stewart, 1989; Marks and Lee, 1989).

2. Greeley (1989) not only reported much lower correlations for Catholic high schools than for public high schools between the academic performance of students and their parents' income and education, but he also found that in Catholic schools, academic performance was virtually uncorrelated with these parent characteristics.

3. Catholic schools were most successful for students whose parents did not attend college and for students who came from lower socioeconomic backgrounds (Bryk and Raudenbush, 1989; Coleman et al., 1982; Coleman and Hoffer, 1987; Greeley, 1982: Lee and

Stewart, 1989; Marks and Lee, 1989). Vitullo-Martin (1979) noted that the same effects occurred in Catholic elementary schools.

4. Sixty-four percent of the white students, 77 percent of the black students, and 66 percent of the Hispanic students in Catholic schools expected to graduate from college. These percentages were from 1.5 to 1.7 times greater than the corresponding percentages of their counterparts in public schools (Greeley, 1982, p. 24). In low-income-serving Catholic schools, 74 percent of the white students, 82 percent of the black students, and 77 percent of the Hispanic students indicated that they thought they had an excellent or good chance of graduating from college (Benson et al., 1986, p. 90).

5. Minority students in Catholic schools are less likely to drop out of school than are minority students in public schools. The findings from *High School and Beyond* demonstrated that Catholic schools had substantially lower dropout rates and higher holding power than did public schools for students typically at a higher risk of dropping out: students from single-parent families, minority students, or students from low-income families.

6. The difference in the likelihood of dropping out for students who were at risk and those who were not at risk was much lower in Catholic schools than in public schools, or even in other private schools (Coleman and Hoffer, 1987). For example, Bryk and Thum (1989) reported that dropout rates are lower in Catholic schools than in public schools, but also that social class is virtually unrelated to dropping out within Catholic schools (pp. 158–59).

My own practice as an urban Catholic school principal during the 1980s and early 1990s confirmed this research on the effectiveness of Catholic schools for minority students, single-parent families, and the poor. The more at risk the child, the more at risk the family, the more effective the Catholic school experience seemed to be. Following Vatican II, Catholic schools were guided by the mandate, "To teach as Jesus did." Thus, in accordance with the principle of unconditional positive regard for all, caring relationships were promoted.

In June of 2004, an interdisciplinary group of twenty-three researchers, educators and government officials met at Wingspread, a conference center in Racine, Wisconsin, to review collectively the literature on the subject of student connection to school and to discuss the impact of "connectedness" upon the academic outcome of students. Together, they published a series of papers and presented the Wingspread Declaration of School Connection, in which they declared that students are more likely to succeed when they feel connected to school. According to their declaration, school connection is the belief by students that adults in the school care about their learning as well as about them as individuals.

Could it be that it is our persistent failure to improve relationships between teachers and students in urban public schools and between urban public schools and minority communities that has caused our persistent inability to empower minority students to reach their full potential within these public schools? There has been ample research and ample evidence to indicate that the answer to this question is yes. We do know what works. We have fine examples of schools that can and do effectively educate all of their students, regardless of race, ethnicity, religion, or economic circumstances. Yet, public schools remain resistant to the wisdom our nation's Catholic schools have to offer.

Thomas Groome, while visiting a Catholic school educator in

Karachi, discovered that there were nearly 550 Catholic schools in Pakistan of various kinds, many of which were huge institutions, providing schooling from kindergarten to college. He was surprised to learn that all of these Catholic schools were predominantly Muslim in faculty and enrollment. Most had less than 5 percent Christian students. He became intrigued by the fact that, although showing none of the trappings of Christianity and providing religious education in Islam, these schools were readily recognized within Pakistani culture as very "different." After careful consideration of this phenomenon, Groome concluded that these schools provide a humanizing curriculum, educating for life for all, and that although the values they reflect cannot be taught overtly from the perspective of Christian faith—as a catechesis—they nevertheless permeate the ethos and style of the schools.

Groome's experience in Pakistan inspired his 1998 book, *Educating for Life: A Spiritual Vision for Every Teacher and Parent*, in which he presents eight substantial characteristics of Catholic Christianity that help weave a spiritual vision of educating for life. According to Groome, these eight characteristics are transferable to all forms of education, whether public, parochial, or homeschooling:

- a positive, benevolent understanding of the human condition;
- a conviction about the sacramentality of life;
- an emphasis on relationships and community;
- a commitment to history and tradition;
- a reflective way of knowing that encourages responsibility and wisdom for life;
- a spiritual focus—seeking the "holiness" of life;
- a commitment to justice and social values of God's reign;

◆ a spirit of catholicity itself—hospitality for all and an openness to truth, wherever it can be found. (pp. 59–60)

Of the eight substantial qualities of Catholic schools identified by Groome, all are highly respectful of the individual, and none carries a price tag. By their very nature, such schools encourage caring relationships, wishing well to the other for his or her own sake. Such relationships have the potential to empower and inspire the other to reach his or her full potential, not only physically and academically, but also emotionally and spiritually—to attain wholeness and fullness of life.

There is no doubt that we have excellent models of schools that offer great hope for the children who languish on the wrong side of the achievement gap. The fact that many of these successful schools are Catholic schools has, for too long, enabled our public school establishment to ignore their wisdom and success. The work of Thomas Groome and John Convey, and the presence of Community of Peace Academy, bear witness to the fact that there is no longer any defensible reason to do so.

CHAPTER 6

I–It to I–Thou

I–it relationships are power based and do not promote moral development. They have no potential for educating for wholeness and fullness of life. Education for wholeness and fullness of life requires I–Thou relationships. Such relationships spring from the response of a free will to a profound sense of belonging.

Historically, the most profound difference between public and Catholic education has been the intended outcome of the educational process. Education of the mind and body—academic and physical education—has been the domain of public education. Education of the whole person—mind, body, and will—has traditionally been left to churches or to private and religiously affiliated schools.

A major aspect of this book is the reconceptualization of the purpose of public education: to educate the whole person—mind, body, and will—for fullness of life for all. Educating a person's will is a moral process. To accomplish this purpose, public schools must be restructured. They must become moral learning communities; communities in which all members strive to make decisions and choices that lead to mental, physical, emotional, and spiritual health and well-being for all. Within such moral learning communities, there is the potential for all to achieve lives that are whole and full.

The education of the human will is new theoretical territory for public education. Therefore, we must look not only to education and sociology but also to theology and philosophy for a theoretical framework.

In *Sharing Faith: A Comprehensive Approach to Religious Education and Pastoral Ministry* (1991), Thomas Groome speaks eloquently of the purpose of religious education as "to bring about the reign of God." According to Groome, "The reign of God must be interpreted within its scriptural meaning of God's covenantal relationship with humankind. In the covenant, what God wills is love and freedom, peace and justice, wholeness and fullness of life for all, favoring the 'lowly' and showing 'no partiality' to the mighty" (p. 15). This definition of the reign of God formed the foundation of the vision statement of Community of Peace Academy, a public charter school: "At Community of Peace Academy, our desired outcome is to educate the whole person—mind, body and will—for peace, justice, freedom, compassion, wholeness and fullness of life for all."

Groome sets forth an ontological pedagogy, a pedagogy that is respectful of the whole person and seeks to educate the whole person. For Groome, the purpose of the educational process is to affirm human beings as the subject of decision. Each person must be free to exercise his or her will; to choose for or against that which is offered. How do we encourage persons to make moral choices of their own free will; choices that lead to mental, physical, emotional, and spiritual well-being for themselves and others?

The works of Aristotle (1925) and Martin Buber (1970) provide insights into the complexities of human relationships as they relate to the shaping of the human will. Aristotle devotes book VIII of *The Nicomachean Ethics* to a discussion of three categories of friendship: friendship for purposes of utility, pleasure, or goodness. Perfect friendships are based upon a goodness that endures.

As an affirmation of Aristotle's categories of friendship, Buber speaks of I–It and I–Thou relationships. When we choose our friends for purposes of utility or pleasure, we create an I–It relationship. The I–Thou relationship wishes well to the other for his or her own sake. In order for us to create schools that are moral learning communities, the relationships within the school must be life giving for all. We must strive for I–Thou relationships.

Michel Foucault paints a grim picture of the ultimate I–It relationship in his book *Discipline and Punish: The Birth of the Prison* (first published in 1975). He discusses "panopticism," an oppressive system by which the prisoner is kept within a circular building called a panopticon. Each cell contains an outside window and a window facing a central guard tower. Light shines into the cell, exposing the prisoner to constant surveillance. Thus, the prisoner is stripped of all human dignity and made a pitiful object, the ultimate It.

Foucault goes on to outline the insidious infiltration of panopticism into all aspects of society. He theorizes that these "panopticisms of every day," as they appear within modern society, join with class domination and become the political counterpart of the norms according to which power is redistributed. Foucault cautions that many of our institutions, including our schools, are thus made impersonal and sometimes inhumane and inhospitable environments.

Too often, public schools have relied upon the panopticisms of every day to manage human relationships and to control behavior through various forms of discipline. Detentions, suspensions, and other purely punitive consequences are examples of this. Such approaches do not encourage students to freely choose goodness. Schools that rely too heavily on such devices frequently have police officers on duty as well; thus, the line between schools and prisons becomes blurred.

While it may be possible to coerce another human being into compliance through the power of discipline, it is not possible to coerce another human being into caring. Caring is a human response to belonging. It is a moral response. Students who feel alienated do not care. Students who do not care are not likely to achieve their full academic potential, nor are they likely to achieve fullness of life.

Within our public schools, our children are too often reduced to things. All relationships become I–It relationships. Nell Noddings (1992) addresses this issue as follows: "Despite our determined optimism and insistent 'everyone-can-do-it,' students complain, 'They don't care!' They suspect that we want their success for our own purposes, to advance our own records, and too often they are right" (p. 13).

According to Michael Apple (1990), "Because schools depend almost exclusively on a statistical model for their normative frame, they generate categories of deviance that are filled with individuals largely from lower socioeconomic groups and ethnic minorities. Thus, the notion of power becomes a critical one" (p. 138).

Parker Palmer (1993) states that "education is the slave of an economic system that wants to master and manipulate nature, society, and even the human heart in order to gain profit and power" (p. 107). Within such an economic system, every relationship becomes an I–It relationship. How do we escape from this? According to Palmer, "Our tendency to blame institutions for our problems is itself a symptom of our objectivism. Institutions are projections of what goes on in the human heart. To ignore the inward sources of our educational dilemmas is only to objectify the problem and thereby multiply it" (p. 107). Our educational dilemmas are moral in nature and we must look inward for solutions.

The issues Foucault, Noddings, Apple, and Palmer raise concern I–It relationships. I–It relationships are power based and do not promote moral development. They have no potential for educating for wholeness and fullness of life. Education for wholeness and fullness of life requires I–Thou relationships. Such relationships spring from the response of a free will to a profound sense of belonging.

If we are to find fullness of life for all, then all of us must be making moral decisions and choices most of the time, of our own free wills. While moral behavior may be taught, it is much more likely to be "caught." Moral behavior cannot be mandated, it must be inspired. Education for wholeness and fullness of life begins in the human heart. It is based upon I–Thou relationships between all members of the community. The adults within the school community must be totally committed to this principle and must be striving to model moral behavior in their own lives, both within and outside of the school community.

Young people will not be fooled. Those who seek to educate the young for wholeness and fullness of life *for all* must act morally. We must create public schools that are moral learning communities where caring, I–Thou relationships are modeled and encouraged. Only within such communities will all students, through positive, moral experiences and relationships, find wholeness and fullness of life for themselves. Only within such moral environments will our nation's future citizens truly learn to care. There is no other way.

EPILOGUE

On June 9, 2004, Tounang Her delivered the following speech at his graduation ceremony at Community of Peace Academy. Tounang's words bear witness to the power of the I–Thou to uplift, inspire, and transform students' lives for the better:

Ua chow, gracias, merci boku, domo arigoto, donkashane. All these words are different in the way they sound, in the way they are written and the countries they come from. But, in the end, they all mean the same thing . . . and that is THANK YOU. And thank you, is exactly what I want to say to my teachers, my friends, and my family. I want to say thank you for always believing in me, for always supporting me and for never giving up on me, even when I had given up on myself.

To my teachers: Mr. Olson, Mr. Fleming and Mr. McGowan, I say thank you. Thank you, and at the same time, I'm sorry. I know at times I was impatient, and during some of those times, I was disrespectful. But, no matter how disrespectful and impatient I was to you, you would always be there when I needed you. Never once did you turn your back on me . . . and I want to thank you for that. I also want to thank you for always believing in me. All those times you guys encouraged me . . . I've kept them with me and I've used them as my fuel to keep going to school. If it wasn't for your encouragement, I don't know if I'd be up here graduating. So, thank you.

To my class, I want to thank you all for supporting me and for always pushing me past my own limitations. You guys are the reason why I am me today, and believe me, I like myself a lot. Seriously, you all helped build my self-confidence and my self-esteem. It's nice to have friends who accept me for who I am. So, thank you for that. I also want to thank you for showing me friendship. You guys have shown me that there is some good in this world . . . that there is something worth living for. You guys have given me hope for myself and for this world. And with that alone, you all have given me the strength to never give up. Thank you.

This school has blessed me with an environment that has helped me grow in so many positive ways. This school and its mission has been a great influence. CPA has given me a new outlook on life and a new outlook on how to live life. It's a great school and I would have never experienced all these things and I would never have learned all the things I've learned, if it wasn't for my Mom and Dad.

Mom and Dad, I want to thank you for forcing me to come to this school. At first I thought it was the worst thing you guys could do to me . . . but, now I realize it's one of the best things you could have done. There's no way I could repay both of you for the things you have done for me, but with this little speech I have written, I just want you *two to know that I do realize all the things both of you have done for me, and I do appreciate all of it. I want to thank both of you for always loving me. Last but not least, I want to thank you guys, the audience, for listening to me. Ua chow, gracias, merci boku, domo arigoto, donkashane. Thank you.*

CHAPTER 7

Choosing Goodness

It is this internal awareness that someone who loves us, someone we care about, is watching that enables us, of our own free will, to live as moral human beings.

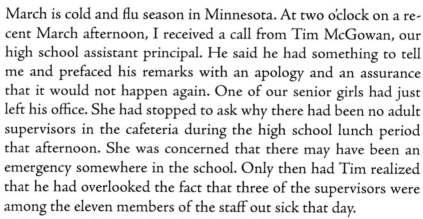

March is cold and flu season in Minnesota. At two o'clock on a re-cent March afternoon, I received a call from Tim McGowan, our high school assistant principal. He said he had something to tell me and prefaced his remarks with an apology and an assurance that it would not happen again. One of our senior girls had just left his office. She had stopped to ask why there had been no adult supervisors in the cafeteria during the high school lunch period that afternoon. She was concerned that there may have been an emergency somewhere in the school. Only then had Tim realized that he had overlooked the fact that three of the supervisors were among the eleven members of the staff out sick that day.

He assured the student that there had been no emergency. He explained that he had been in a meeting with me and had been sur-prised when he checked his watch and realized that he had missed the high school lunch. He had not realized, until she called it to his attention, that all the supervisors had been missing. The student assured him that in the absence of the supervisors the seniors had taken over. Since they weren't sure who was on the cleaning crew that day, they had cleaned the tables and floors and dismissed the students back to their classes. Upon checking later with the women who work in the kitchen, we learned that they were unaware that the adult supervisors were missing.

Community of Peace Academy was founded upon the premise that public schools must be about the business of educating the human will for moral goodness; to prove the possibility, the necessity, and the effectiveness of educating public school children for wholeness and fullness of life for all. The academy was established upon the premise that one had a free will and that one could never be truly educated against one's will. Further, it was based upon the understanding that goodness matters; that a well-educated person who is evil is a greater threat to society than an undereducated person who is good.

The principles upon which this public charter school was founded, though profoundly Judeo-Christian in character, are broadly applicable. They have potential to transform lives for the better. They are principles essential to creating and sustaining peaceful moral communities, including school communities.

Amitai Etzioni (1993) reminds us that the only way the moral integrity of a society can be preserved is for most of the people, most of the time, to abide by their commitments voluntarily. He states that the disciplinary powers of government should be called upon only as a last resort to deal with the small number of sociopaths and hard-core recalcitrants, those who do not have moral commitments or sufficient impulse control to heed those commitments. Likewise, the only way the moral integrity of a school can be preserved is for most of the students, most of the time, to abide by their commitments voluntarily.

Learning to become a moral human being is a lifelong process. A moral person must make decisions and choices, most of the time, of his or her own free will, that lead to mental, emotional, physical, and spiritual health and well-being for self *and for others*. Morality, as it is defined here, requires the practice of unconditional positive regard for the other and the I–Thou relationships that result from this. Care of the other requires humility, forgiveness, and the ability to empathize with the other, to see things from another's perspective. Human beings do not do these things naturally. Yet, if we hope to find inner peace, if we hope to live together in peace, most of us, by the time we become adults, must be well on our way to becoming moral human beings.

Where do our moral commitments come from? How do we ensure that our youth will embrace the moral commitments essential to their own well-being and the well-being of others? Where do the young—where indeed do any of us—gain the impulse control required for moral conduct? Those who have accepted the high calling of educating our nation's children must search for the truth regarding the answers to such questions.

Michel Foucault (1977) wrestled with questions regarding morality and the free will. Within Foucault's panopticon, light illuminates the activity of the prisoners so that the eye in the tower can observe them constantly. When asked if the eye in the tower was the eye of God, Foucault remarked, "it is a totally malevolent eye."

Human beings seem to require some *watchful eye* to assist them in behaving morally and ethically. For children, it is most often the eye of a watchful parent. As we grow to be morally responsible adults, we either internalize the eye of our parent or we replace or supplement it with the eye of a substitute "parent," or a transcendent parent or "higher power." It is this internal awareness that someone who loves us, someone we care about, is watching that enables us, of our own free will, to live as moral human beings. We often refer to this watchful eye as the conscience. Those who do not internalize a caring, loving "watchful eye" frequently find themselves under the constant surveillance of an uncaring and impersonal eye—perhaps, ultimately, a parole officer or prison guard.

Whether the watchful eye that directs our moral lives is malevolent or loving will have a profound impact upon the wholeness and fullness of life we achieve. It will also profoundly affect the way we treat others. For the good of all, our desire must be that our children grow and mature as citizens beneath a watchful eye that is loving. We must strive to assure that all of our nation's children live in the I–Thou most of the time.

When we are children, we must sometimes be forced, against our will, to comply with our parents' wishes. If our parents are loving, they must, from time to time, intervene in our willfulness, to keep us from harming ourselves or others. Our childish decisions to eat the whole plate of cookies, to pull the cat by its tail, or to hit our brother over the head with our truck, would not be in anyone's best interest. As we grow up within a loving, caring family, our love for our parents, the cat, and our brothers and sisters grows. We begin to internalize the moral values of those who love us and to make moral decisions more and more often out of love and care for them. We care; therefore, we act morally.

This natural process of moral development is jeopardized whenever a primary relationship in the life of a child is interrupted. Divorce, addictions, mental and physical illnesses, unplanned pregnancies, incarceration, and various kinds of child abuse are among factors that can sever or severely strain primary parent–child relationships, thus profoundly impacting children's lives. These wounded, broken children bring their anger, emptiness, anxiety, and frustrations to school. Having failed to internalize the watchful eye of a loving parent to assist them in making moral decisions and choices, they may appear not to care about themselves or others. Such problems have an effect on the lives of countless children whose alienation and emptiness are further exacerbated by the loss of community in our contemporary society.

I attended grade school in a small town on the South Dakota prairie. As in most such towns, everyone knew everyone. Wherever I went, watchful eyes were upon me. They were the eyes of my parents' friends and of my friends' parents. They were friendly eyes. Their benevolent gaze joined the watchful eyes of my parents and further inspired me to make positive decisions and choices.

In 1955, when my family moved to the west side of St. Paul, Minnesota, I was in the sixth grade. In those days, St. Paul, like many cities, was a series of small neighborhoods, each with a distinct small-town feel and character. Our school was the center of our neighborhood. We all walked home for lunch. There were small stores on many of the corners we crossed. We knew the names of the shopkeepers, and they knew our names.

Most of us went to church on Sunday. We attended various Orthodox, Catholic, and Protestant churches scattered throughout our community. Wherever we went, we saw people we knew. For the most part, my friends and I were being raised under a common set of values. The watchful eyes that joined those of our parents, and our various interpretations of God in guiding our wills, were benevolent, familiar eyes.

During my lifetime, the United States has begun to lose its neighborhoods and communities. Many people have no idea who their neighbors are. Many cities have lost the concept of neighborhood schools. We shop in enormous, impersonal stores and seldom see anyone we know. Strangers often fail to acknowledge one another in any way. The excessive use of cell phones has made it likely that people we meet while shopping, waiting in line, or passing on the street will truly not even see us. For children, the pervasive anonymity of modern life often means that no one is really watching.

For too many children, all relationships are I–It relationships. At home, at school and within their communities, they find no one to offer them unconditional love. Every child must have at least one person who loves him or her unconditionally. Without this love, one simply does not care about the outcome of one's decisions and choices. Harming self and others is of little consequence to someone who moves through life feeling anonymous; whose worth has never been validated by the I–Thou relationship. Such children would benefit from the knowledge that they are absolutely unique and precious to God, who created them and loves them unconditionally.

Within our nation's public schools, that life-changing message can only be delivered through our human actions. It is a message that hundreds of thousands of our public school children need to internalize in order to become moral human beings; in order to find wholeness and fullness of life. If they are to reach their full potential, children must first be affirmed as the "Thou." They must know, at a deeply personal level, that they are absolutely loved and valued, without condition. For many, until this happens, reaching the proficiency level on state tests will remain an illusion.

Our nation's public schools are failing to address this critical issue. America's current education agenda is flawed. If we are sincere in wanting every child to succeed, then we must address each one as the Thou. We must create, within our public schools, highly supportive and caring moral learning communities, in which unconditional positive regard for all is practiced. Within such communities, our children may internalize a loving watchful eye. Thus validated and affirmed, all public school students, regardless of race, creed, or economic status, may be empowered and inspired to freely choose goodness, the solid foundation of a life that is whole and full.

CHAPTER 8

Going Public

During my sixteen years as a non-Catholic participant observer in Catholic education, I learned a great deal. It was clear to me that the foundational principles underlying Catholic education were effective, particularly in the education of children who, like my own sons and my former students, often fail to thrive in public schools. I also suspected that these foundational principles were transferable to any kind of education, including public education.

I was born into a Lutheran home in the 1940s and for most of my youth attended Holy Trinity Evangelical Lutheran Church on the west side of St. Paul, the church that had been founded by my great-grandfather, Reverend A. J. D. Haupt. My parents met in the Luther League at Holy Trinity, and I was baptized, confirmed, and had been married there. I attended public schools from kindergarten through high school and graduated from Gustavus Adolphus, a Swedish Lutheran college in St. Peter, Minnesota.

The unlikely circumstance that led me to Catholic education and to the discovery of a new vision for America's public schools happened in 1976. That summer, I found myself, a recently divorced single mother with two young sons, without a teaching position owing to a massive layoff in the St. Paul Public Schools. I was desperate for a job, and so, with some reluctance, I accepted a position offered by the district that did not require my teaching degree. I was assigned to two Catholic grade schools, one serving the African American community in the Summit–University area and one serving the Mexican American community on Saint Paul's west side. My title was home-school liaison, and I would assist these schools with their desegregation efforts under a federal Title IV grant. Prior to that unlikely assignment, I knew nothing about Catholic education, nor had I ever been inside a Catholic school.

What I found in the Catholic grade schools to which the district assigned me made an immediate and lasting impression. I noticed that everyone seemed deeply committed to the educational process and to one another. Everyone seemed to be "on the same page." While Catholic schools seemed open to new pedagogical ideas, there was a shared philosophy, mission, and vision that were not subject to change. Those involved in the enterprise knew why they were there, and they knew that the outcome would be positive for the students. They knew this because they had a history of delivering education in this way over a long period of time, and they had witnessed their success. They had seen many generations of their students reach wholeness and fullness of life.

During my sixteen years as a non-Catholic participant observer in Catholic education, I learned a great deal. It was clear to me that the foundational principles underlying Catholic education were effective, particularly in the education of children who, like my own sons and my former students, often fail to thrive in public schools. I also suspected that these foundational principles were transferable to any kind of education, including public education.

In 1991, the Minnesota legislature passed the first charter school law in America. Fueled by cries for reform and the desire by liberals to quiet conservative demands for vouchers, this new legislation made it possible to found public schools that would be treated as independent public school districts. Charter schools would be given autonomy in return for results. Each school would be governed by its own board of directors. The Minnesota charter school law required that teachers have the controlling vote on these teacher–parent boards, a concept that made teachers the management, thus diminishing the need for union influence.

While studying at the University of St. Thomas in 1993, I was introduced to the work of Thomas Groome. As a Catholic school principal, I was able to participate in the Murray Institute, a tuition-free program for archdiocesan principals and directors of religious education programs. Groome's book *Sharing Faith* (1991) became the focus of two semesters of study. This landmark work profoundly influenced faith formation programs in Catholic schools and parishes across the country.

Our professor, Sister Mary Katherine Hamilton, went to great lengths to challenge us to apply these concepts broadly—to see that they pertained not only to Christian education but to all education. She stated that Groome's approach was a model that could lead to wisdom in any educational setting. At the time, I found her challenge interesting. I would soon see it as prophetic.

In May of 1994, shortly after resigning my position as a Catholic school principal, I was offered the opportunity to cofound a public charter school. Mike Ricci, who would be my partner, had been active in school choice initiatives for many years. He was a proponent of vouchers and had lobbied for the charter school law. His experience and connections would be invaluable in overcoming the legal and business hurdles of the chartering process. As an educator, I would assist by developing the educational program for the school.

The urban Catholic school formed the blueprint for this public school reform effort. We would attempt to educate not only the mind and body but also the human will. The work of Thomas Groome proved foundational in determining how one might approach the education of the human will in a secular setting. Groome (1991) introduced the concept of an ontological pedagogy, one that involved the whole person—mind, body and will. He described five "movements" toward shared Christian praxis that are applicable to all of teaching:

- Movement 1: Naming/Expressing "Present Praxis"
- Movement 2: Critical Reflection on Present Action
- Movement 3: Making Accessible the Christian Story and Vision
- Movement 4: Dialectical Hermeneutic of Appropriate Christian Story/Vision to Participants' Stories/Visions
- Movement 5: Decision/Response for Lived Christian Faith

In a public school setting, the Christian story and vision in Movement 3 would be replaced with other stories of an ethical/moral nature. In Movement 4, students would be challenged to place their critical understanding of their present practice in dialogue with the new story/vision, and to attempt to interpret the new material and come to terms with its meaning for their lives. This is the dialectical hermeneutic of which Groome speaks.

Of critical importance would be the point of decision in Movement 5. This is the point at which the student is challenged to choose, of his or her own free will, whether to accept the new story/vision that has been presented. This point of "moral decision making" has the potential to shape the human will.

There were other challenges. The fact that Catholic schools were Roman Catholic was an essential factor in their success that could not be ignored. First, this quality gave the schools a philosophical focus. They were Roman Catholic institutions, guided by ancient principles. Everyone knew what the bottom line was. Everyone was on the same page. This philosophical focus was the thing that had most impressed me about Catholic schools from the start. It provided a sense of direction, purpose, and peace that I had found missing in public schools.

Second, this strong Christian focus provided a common set of values upon which the members of the community, for the most part, agreed. These values were taught daily as part of the curriculum. Further, it was assumed that the adults in the school were committed to these values and were striving to practice them in their own lives. Since values are most often "caught" from members of one's community, this was a great advantage in passing them on to children.

One could not deny that these decidedly Christian elements were important in creating the positive school culture I had grown to appreciate during my years as a Catholic school teacher and principal. While I was not entirely sure that it would be possible to create a similarly effective learning environment without them, I had come to believe that many of the key elements that made Catholic schools effective were not of a religious nature. It was these that I would identify and attempt to replicate.

At the same time, my faith was important to me. I had always defined my professional work in terms of my faith. From the beginning, teaching had been my *calling*, my response to God's goodness and presence in my life. I found my answer to this dilemma in the words of St. Francis of Assisi: "Preach the Gospel always, and if necessary, use words." This would be the key. We would need to rely upon our actions and the example of our lives to create a moral public school community.

Inspired by the challenge, we set to work writing the proposal for this public school. The importance of "community" to the success of Catholic schools had been well documented. It had also been my experience that the support of the parish greatly enhanced the work of Catholic educators and supported the success of Catholic school students. I had observed the many ways in which involvement in the life of the school and parish positively impacted the families of our students. As I contemplated my future, I personally grieved the loss of "parish" and wondered if I would ever again experience the level of love and support that I had known as a Catholic school principal. How could we build a caring, supportive community within a new public school? This would certainly need to be a major priority and focus.

The name of the school was chosen carefully. Due to increased activity of street gangs during the late 1980s and early 1990s, violence had been on the increase in the city of Minneapolis. Once an oasis in the midst of the storm, violence eventually reached the doors of the small Catholic school where I served as principal: One student witnessed the shooting of her uncle in his apartment. Another student's father was stabbed with a screwdriver. A third student was wounded in a random gang shooting outside his cousin's home; he was told he would never again walk.

Violence was closing in on all of us. In response to this, peace became the focus of our new public school. We would call it Community of Peace Academy. We would intentionally teach and practice conflict prevention and ethical behavior. Nonviolence would be modeled by the staff and practiced by all members of our school community.

To foster the development of meaningful relationships and a caring community over time, the charter school would serve grades K through 8. It would be small so that no matter how many needs our students and their families might have, we could find the time and resources to assist them. Teachers would have the same students for two years in a row, not just one. This would enable teachers to know their students and families well. We would make visits to the homes of every student every year to help build trust between teachers and parents. Class sizes would be limited to no more than twenty-four. Time would be set aside every day to build relationships and trust within classrooms and for teaching peace and ethics as part of our curriculum.

Discipline would not be punitive; rather, it would be restorative. The concept of "respect" as a value had been somewhat tainted by the influence of gangs. Within gang culture, "dissing," showing disrespect, could bring severe retaliation. Inspired by Nell Noddings (1994), we decided that our code of conduct would instead be called the Code of Caring Behaviors. It would be based upon caring rather than respect:

> *I will care for myself,*
> *I will care for others,*
> *I will care for things,*
> *I will care for learning,*
> *I will care for the environment.*

We would not use detention. We would minimize suspensions. Parents would be our equal partners as members of a Resolution Committee that would meet with students to write behavior contracts. We would work as a team in assisting students to improve their behavior. Peace Circles would replace morning prayer as a time to share joys and concerns and offer support when needed. Time would be set aside each day to actively teach positive values. Research led to an abundance of suitable curriculum for teaching values, all of which had been written for public schools.

The charter school law required that charter developers seek approval from the school board in the district in which the new school would be located. In December of 1994, we presented our proposal to the St. Paul Public School Board. The chair of the board, having read the proposal, remarked that this was the kind of school any parent would want for their child. She was concerned, however, that we might be seeking the "cream of the crop." A second meeting was held to assure the board that it was in fact our intention to reach the students who historically have not found success in public schools—those who might appreciate the option of a smaller and more personal education, but could not pay the tuition that might give them access to private or parochial schools. In the end, the proposal was unanimously approved. A member of the board remarked that it was the first time in recent history that the St. Paul Board of Education had voted unanimously on anything—a sign of things to come.

Leadership for Fullness of Life for All

Sister Pat's example, and my own experience as a Catholic school principal, had provided the perfect model of leadership for this new public
charter school. I would need to be a servant-leader. Everyone would need
to be treated with unconditional positive regard.

It was while working in Catholic schools that I began to realize
the potential of leadership for good or for ill. As a public school
teacher, I had learned to tolerate administration. The principal was
a distant authority figure. Mandates came from on high and were
often ignored. Early on, I was aware that much money and time
were being wasted on new public school initiatives that few teachers took seriously. Whether taken seriously or not, each initiative
was soon replaced by another.

During my first teaching assignment, I came to think of the
principal as a person who sat in his office and tried to think of
things for me to do that would distract me from my teaching. In
my annual review, the principal noted that I was usually late for
meetings. It was true. I perceived meetings to be a waste of my
valuable time and always tried to finish just one more purposeful
task before leaving my classroom.

The next principal I encountered was young and handsome,
and it was rumored that he was romantically involved with one

of the teachers. During my short tenure in his building, it was decided that the entire first floor and second floor would change places. I don't remember why. On the day of the move, he was out of the building. Any respect I may have had for him dissipated by the end of that very stressful and taxing day.

Upon request, I was allowed to transfer to a new magnet school the next year. The principal was a seasoned veteran who had been chosen to open what was to be a model program. The high visibility and politics of this endeavor created a stressful environment for everyone in the first year. This principal was hands-on and intimidating. His presence on our floor caused a sense of panic among my colleagues.

It was in 1976 that I was assigned to two Catholic schools as a home-school liaison. There I encountered a new style of school administration in the persons of two Catholic nuns: Sister Anne and Sister Pat. Both were small, unassuming women. In fact, at four feet, eight inches, Sister Pat was tiny. These women administered different schools in different parts of the city, but their style of leadership was the same. They were welcoming and approachable. They were known by students and enjoyed students. Their demeanor was peaceful and calm. They seemed genuinely happy with their work and genuinely interested in others.

The following year, Sister Pat offered me a teaching position and I gladly accepted. As a single parent with two small sons, I was grateful to be working in a caring environment. Life was a challenge. At this Catholic school, I was not merely the teacher in room 103. Sister Pat saw and appreciated my strengths, but she also acknowledged my needs as a human being. One cold winter day I arrived at school late because my car wouldn't start. I was amazed and filled with gratitude when, instead of chastising me, Sister Pat covered my class and sent me to Sears for a new battery. On another occasion, when I was particularly overwhelmed with the realities of my life as full-time teacher and single parent, this principal instructed me to forget about grading papers for one night and get some rest!

Being a member of a caring, responsive educational community during those difficult years was a blessing for which I will always be grateful. The same care that was extended to me was also extended to others. Teachers, parents, and students were acknowledged with unconditional positive regard. This was a diverse school community, both racially and economically. Sister Pat honored all of us equally. Her example set the tone.

Sister Pat was a mediator. During my third year, I switched grades and subjects. I was teaching fourth grade, and math was my specialty. About midyear, one of the parents became concerned that I was not challenging her son in math. My attempts to address her concerns were not successful, and her tone became increasingly hostile. The situation was causing me worry and stress. Sister Pat arranged a meeting for the three of us. Passing time has erased from memory the content of our conversation, but I will always remember the flowers and the message of reconciliation that arrived the next day from the parent.

Sister Pat's ability to bring out the best in everyone was one of her greatest strengths. She always noticed people's "gifts" and used them to enrich the community. I am a perfectionist and so have a tendency to prefer doing things myself. Sister Pat taught me the importance of allowing others to participate, even though the result may sometimes not live up to one's own standard. When people's contributions are sought out and appreciated, they are often inspired to become more than they ever imagined they could be. Contributing members feel a true sense of ownership. Ownership builds community.

Under Sister Pat's administration, leadership was not about what "I" want, it was about what "we" want. She always consulted the troops. Hiring was a group enterprise. Anyone who was interested could participate in hiring new teachers. Decisions regarding curriculum were made by everyone and supported by everyone. New initiatives took hold and bore fruit.

The staff had fun together. I learned that Catholic nuns enjoy a good time. Great attention was paid to parties and celebrations. These special times came often. They drew us together in a true spirit of community and made us all feel appreciated and cared for.

Of the many lessons she taught me, the most valuable was the lesson of humility. Sister Pat put herself at our service. She lived Christ's example. Daily, she *washed our feet*. If there was work to be done, she would be the first to step forward. She picked up trash, carried things, helped set up and take down, cleaned tables, and swept floors. She would bring us coffee and clean up after us. She was a servant-leader, and we loved to follow her.

During my fifth year at this Catholic school, Sister Pat accepted a call to a parish school in south Minneapolis. One of the teachers, a young woman who had been, but was no longer, a nun, took her place. Under Miss Cathy's administration, the same caring spirit prevailed. When she married the following year, the school was to hire a principal with a very different style.

The new principal kept her distance. She preferred to communicate by memo. Decisions were made behind closed doors with little input from those affected. Slowly, the ethos of the school began to change. Discontent breeds unhappiness. Unhappy people think more of themselves than of others. The community we had known was in jeopardy.

In February of her second year, the new principal was asked to leave. The board approached the staff and asked if any of us would be willing to serve as principal for the rest to the school year. I raised my hand. This was to be my unexpected introduction to school administration. I followed Sister Pat's example to the best of my ability. Within weeks, our caring school community had been restored.

The following year, I resigned my teaching position and began my studies in nonpublic school administration at the University of St. Thomas. My goal was to become a Catholic school principal. Before my graduation in July of 1986, I had been hired to administer a small Catholic grade school in south Minneapolis, where, for the next seven years, Sister Pat and I would serve together on the Inner Urban Catholic Coalition School Committee.

By the spring of 1994, I had administered urban Catholic grade schools for a total of eight years and felt it was time to move on. A week after my resignation, I was offered the opportunity to co-found a public charter school. I would spend the next year preparing the proposal and promoting the new school to the public.

During my tenure as principal there, Holy Name Catholic School in south Minneapolis had become accredited through the Minnesota Nonpublic School Accrediting Association (MNSAA). In order to become accredited, the staff of each school in the MNSAA was required to spend a year conducting a comprehensive self-study and writing an extensive report about their school. Once the self-study report was submitted, the association would send a team of MNSAA members to conduct a site visit. The purpose of these visits was to validate the strengths and areas of need identified in each school's report, and to ensure that they were true to their stated mission.

Having been a member of MNSAA for six years, I had served on many validation teams. During the 1994–1995 school year, while working on the proposal for the new charter school, I continued working for MNSAA and chaired the validation teams for three schools. These were rewarding and enlightening experiences.

Through my work with MNSAA, it became apparent to me that successful schools were successfully governed. If a school was in turmoil, it often had to do with governance issues. When the person at the top, be it priest or principal, was not consultative and insisted upon over ruling board members and/or staff members on significant issues, trust would be lacking and the morale in the school would be low. In these situations, factions would often be at work, resulting in various degrees of dysfunction. In schools where all were treated with unconditional positive regard, morale would be high, trust would prevail, and the school would be functioning as a caring supportive community of learners.

When I first read Minnesota's new charter school law, it was clear that governance would be a challenge. Administration had been overlooked. Nowhere in the law was reference made to the role of principal. Having been a principal for the past eight years, and having gained great respect for the importance of effective school leadership, this oversight concerned me. I was intending to be the principal of the school I was founding. Could a charter school hire a principal? I wasn't entirely sure that there would be a place for me in this new school.

Upon further investigation, I learned that the charter school legislation was written to empower teachers and parents to run their own schools. Since I was a teacher with lifetime certification in the state of Minnesota, I was qualified to open a charter school. I also learned that charter schools were free to hire administrators.

In Minnesota, Charter schools are nonprofit organizations run by a board and executive director. In the nonprofit world, the executive director is hired and supervised by the board. The executive is empowered to run the nonprofit, in this case, the school, on behalf of the board. This includes full responsibility for the hiring and supervision of staff. Based upon my past experience, I determined that, in such case, the executive director needed to be the principal.

Of equal interest were legislative requirements regarding the structure of charter school boards. The law stated that teachers must have the majority vote on these governing boards. This was a model that I had never before encountered. Parents and parishioners served on Catholic school boards. In my experience, teachers did not sit on the boards of Catholic schools, nor did teachers traditionally sit on the boards of private or public schools. It was equally uncommon for employees to serve on nonprofit boards.

As I thought about these things, it occurred to me that in such a school, the teachers who served on the board would be empowered to hire, supervise, and, if necessary, dismiss the executive director/principal who would be empowered to hire, supervise, and, if necessary, dismiss them. It was obvious that to function effectively, this unique governance model would call for the highest possible level of moral integrity on the part of everyone.

Sister Pat's example, and my own experience as a Catholic school principal, had provided the perfect model of leadership for this new public charter school. I would need to be a servant-leader. Everyone would need to be treated with unconditional positive regard. Most important, such leadership had the potential to inspire and empower all members of the school community to freely choose fullness of life for all.

PART III

Community of Peace Academy

~

Consider the worthiest purpose of education as that learners might become fully alive human beings, who help to create a society that serves the common good.

THOMAS GROOME,
*EDUCATING FOR LIFE: A SPIRITUAL VISION
FOR EVERY TEACHER AND PARENT*

CHAPTER 10

Seeking Wise People

An application process was developed in which candidates were sent a copy of the vision, mission, and philosophy of Community of Peace Academy, along with a letter describing the school and the position for which they were applying. They were asked to reflect upon the founding documents and to respond in writing by telling what they most agreed with and why. They were asked why they wanted to be a part of this particular school community, and, following sister Pat's lead, they were asked what special "gifts" they would bring to the school. From the beginning, all members of the staff have been hired in this way.

⟶

The reason I first applied to Community of Peace Academy, was because of first, the name of the school. That got my attention in the want ads, and then when I sent for the application and I got the four essay question application, it just knocked my socks off, because I had just filled out literally, I think I applied to seven districts in the state, and they were just these huge applications of: fill in the blanks and where have you lived in the last ten years and what is your teaching experience for the past ten years, what was your income, you know, all of those questions. But then, I received the application from Community of Peace Academy, which didn't care anything about your middle name and date of birth, and just got to the four core questions. And I spent all day writing it and had the best time of my life, because it was actually . . . somebody was asking me for what I

*really . . . what I thought and what I believed in. It was the first time
anyone had asked me.*

     —*Rob White, Community of Peace Academy Teacher*

It was during my very first teaching assignment that I came to respect the power of teachers in determining the success or failure
of new initiatives. As I watched new initiatives come and go, it was
clear that unless an initiative had the full support of staff, which
was hardly ever the case, it would not survive. Once the proposal
for Community of Peace Academy was written, I was aware that
unless I hired staff members who understood and believed in the
vision, mission, and philosophy of the school, these written statements would never become a reality.

In early spring of 1995, a copy of the entire proposal was sent to
directors of the education departments of select colleges and uni-
versities, along with a letter requesting that they forward it to students who might be especially interested and qualified. However,
it was not practical to send the entire proposal to all prospective
candidates. An application process was developed in which candidates were sent a copy of the vision, mission, and philosophy of
Community of Peace Academy, along with a letter describing the
school and the position for which they were applying. They were
asked to reflect upon these founding documents and to respond
in writing by telling what they most agreed with and why. They
were asked why they wanted to be a part of this *particular* school
community, and, following sister Pat's lead, they were asked what
special "gifts" they would bring to the school. From the beginning,
all members of the staff have been hired in this way.

As many as fifty of these application packets might be sent out,
and as few as five returned. Each time, applications received tend
to be thoughtfully written and the candidates of an unusually high
quality.

When asked what attracts them to this particular position, candidates for employment at Community of Peace Academy nearly always say that they are attracted by the name of the school and by its philosophy and mission. There is no shortage of quality educators who are looking for something noble to commit their lives to. Following are excerpts from the application essays of current employees.

I visited the school for one of my classes at Hamline University in Spring 2004 and was immediately impressed with its objective and mission. I want to work at Community of Peace Academy in particular, because I am certain my philosophical agreement with the school will make it easier for me to help students succeed.

Along those same lines, I am confident that working in a school I am philosophically aligned with will help me better understand my own identity as a teacher, as a person and as a lifetime student. This reason might be the most significant, if only because an educator is most effective when he or she understands her- or himself. I strongly believe Community of Peace will help me better understand myself.

The aspect of the philosophy I agree with the most is creating a peaceful environment. Once students are in an environment that feels safe to them, they can turn their focus to learning and doing their personal best.

I have taught at Community of Peace Academy before and loved it. As I took the year off to complete my education and observed in different public schools, I realized that I miss the environment here. All the staff were really caring of one another and respected one another. Bottom line, the staff also practiced what they were teaching the students. The most important thing an adult can do for a child is to model what he/she teaches. If we want to teach students the skills they need in order to succeed in life, whether it be peace and ethics or subject knowledge, then we as adults must show them that we are using those exact skills as adults.

I worked at a culturally diverse school in Japan for over twenty years and experienced first hand the benefits of diversity. Children learn to value other cultures and also learn that people who may be different from themselves have the same needs, feelings and challenges.

I believe that teachers must be models. I can't teach reading if I don't read. I can't teach kids not to smoke if I smoke. Children will only learn to be compassionate if they see compassion acted out in their teachers, parents, and older siblings.

Teachers need to address the larger issues beyond academics such as character and emotional and spiritual growth. It isn't enough for a teacher to teach content; a teacher must also teach how to live life fully in a balanced way so that the students will contribute to their friends, family, and community and the larger society.

I appreciate the emphasis in the statement of beliefs on high expectations and encouragement. Those two words characterize my teaching style. I believe that all children can accomplish if they are encouraged and the task is designed to fit their interests and ability level. I helped an ESL student write a five page history paper on Justinian by using encouragement and careful guidance. The student contributed the hard work and we both experienced the success.

Too often, students are educated to pass certain tests or based upon the teacher's expertise. This leaves out educating the whole child. It is important for young students to get an education not only for academic success, but for success outside the classroom. It is the responsibility of

educators to educate the whole child. If the whole student can be educated, test results and academic success will follow.

～

My response to question number one may not meet your expectations because the schools where I attended as a child were much different from those of the United States. However, the philosophy is different but the mission is similar to the one of the Community of Peace Academy. The difference is that the schools in Laos operated only under the government, and parents and community have no voices and involvement. Also, in Laos the schools are the primary teachers of the students. At Community of Peace Academy it is very open; it allows the parents and community to have the opportunity to really be involved and voice their opinions which empowers the parents to be part of their child's education.

～

Your belief that "racial and cultural diversity within our educational settings expands our world view and enriches our education" resonates with me most profoundly. It is obvious from reading your Student-Family Profile that this is a belief you actively practice. I might add, that judging from the number of students who receive free and/or reduced priced meals, your school also believes in economic diversity.

I agree that such diversity is a valuable asset to a school. It is only when we get to know people from backgrounds other than our own that we have the impetus and awareness necessary to understand our world from different points of view. This awareness has the potential to expand not only our immediate compassion for others, but our understanding of history, politics, economics and psychology as well, because now we are able to see a particular situation from a different perspective. Having this depth of understanding is essential in our quest for world peace.

I bring to your school a very strong academic background in and knowledge of the issues facing people who are not of the dominant culture in our society. My work at Pacific Oaks College taught me to see the incredible pervasiveness of racist, sexist, classist and homophobic practices in our society. From my work as a teacher, I also know first hand how these issues affect the classroom and how they must be actively addressed for progress to be made.

➣

In my experience, I have found that a strong relationship between teachers and parents, as well as between the learning community and parents, is extremely beneficial to student learning. I believe that teachers and parents enter into a partnership in the learning community. I also feel that parents appreciate being a part of their student's education, and students are more likely to learn and grow under the encouragement of parents and teachers together.

➣

I strongly agree with the statement that "Racial and cultural diversity within our school community expands our world view and enriches our education." Children learn through experiences. While children come to school in order to gain academic knowledge, they also need to learn how to be caring and productive participants in a diverse community. This aspect of a child's education is necessary in order to adequately prepare them for an enriching and successful life.

➣

While all schools likely aim for peaceful students, few actively teach to produce them. Fewer still focus on this goal year-round, every year in every class and every school function. But since peacefulness is such a critical ingredient to social success, it only makes sense to do so, for lim-

ited effort always produces limited results. If nonviolence is not a school-wide and consistent objective, we will never decrease the violent instincts of individuals, institutions and, unfortunately, some countries.

That might be enough to justify my desire to work at *Community of Peace Academy*, but there is much more to be excited about. The school also focuses on whole person education, which I take to be a self-evident benefit to individuals and society as well. While all schools educate students' bodies and minds, too many public schools seem to pretend that spirituality does not exist when it most clearly does, albeit in many different forms.

That *Community of Peace* spends time discussing this facet of the human condition can only benefit students, so long as one particular spirituality is not preached. It took me many years of study and independent research to understand how important my personal spirituality was to my own happiness, but I wonder if I would have reached that realization more quickly had I attended a public school that openly communicated about this ingredient of life. If I had realized the importance of spirituality earlier, how might my life be different?

As a person who values diversity in all its forms, I am attracted to your school's stance that a diverse community of students, staff and parents enriches one's education. As a person of color growing up in the suburbs I stood out in a sea of white faces. While doing various jobs in the St. Paul District as a college student, I began to see how beautiful diverse faces are. The cultural differences serve to expand everyone's view of the world. Now as a prospective teacher, I am committed to working in an environment that is racially, ethnically and culturally diverse and in one that celebrates those differences.

A strength I would bring is my presence as a role model. I would be a positive example for students to see every day. I would model peace building and nonviolent practices in my personal and classroom environments. As a woman of color I would act as a living example that *anything is possible for them; that it doesn't matter what color you are or what your background is.*

What I most agree with about the mission statement, is the idea that education happens in relationships. Today I went on a little research adventure and found your school very appealing. I drove through the east side of St. Paul to locate the school and happened upon a car wash being sponsored by the high school student council. While my car was being washed, I had the opportunity to ask students about the school. The responses were faces lighting up with "its a great school." I heard wonderful things about the teen nights and after school activities for kids. The staff member on hand with the group was just as positive and welcoming. He spoke proudly of the school community, the mission, teaching philosophy and academic results. Also, before I ventured to the car wash, I saw a young man mowing the school lawn and I stopped to ask him about the school. He too was very polite and talked about the close-knit staff.

Well, needless to say, my unscientific survey and poll was 100% positive! I am certain your school faces challenges, but I am genuinely interested in being a part of a school that is so described by the people who are part of it.

I agree that teaching our students to interact with one another in a violence free environment is imperative for safe and successful learning. In the past decade, violence has claimed the lives of many and devastated families, schools, and communities, in my country and elsewhere, and it is time that we, as teachers and parents, do something about it. Also, our world is becoming more diverse, therefore, it gives our students an advantage when we teach them how to be accepting and respectful of other cultures, races, and ethnicities.

Having come from Lebanon, a different and very diverse culture, and having learned to speak four languages, I hope to teach the students how to appreciate living, learning, and communicating with individuals of different cultural, racial, and ethnic backgrounds. Also having been an ESL student, I would bring my experience and perspective to enhance the students' learning. Finally, I hope to share my solid knowledge of the content areas as well as strategies on how to study them.

Students, particularly in urban settings, experience much that can be distracting, disturbing, and potentially harmful. I know, because I live in Minneapolis and my own children have always attended urban schools. Clearly the Board of Community of Peace Academy is committed to success for all by focusing on the education of the whole person. As a teacher, I am also fully committed to educating the whole person— mind, body and will—within a peaceful, respectful environment.

During my college experience, I had the opportunity to complete my student teaching in England, which led to further employment for the remainder of the academic year. Throughout this experience, I was able to teach in a culturally and racially diverse community of students and staff, and it has encouraged and inspired me to continue in such a setting. I feel it expands the academic experience and allows for a more enriching education. I strongly believe in Community of Peace Academy's mission statement, and would be honored to contribute to the commitment I have experienced among the staff and students while substitute teaching here.

I have lived in St. Paul for twenty years and feel it's important to serve the community I live in. It is my greatest hope to work as a teacher in the city. I visited your school when I dropped off my application materials and found it to be a beautiful space. This may sound strange, but I do think physical space speaks greatly of an organization. The school immediately impressed me; I found it welcoming and open. Overall, though, I am attracted to the philosophy of the school. It is clear in reading your materials that the student is at the center of all your concerns. It is important to me that students are allowed to direct their learning. My classroom will be open to each student's specific needs and hopes. Those needs and hopes will direct all of the work, play, and daily practices. I feel Community of Peace supports that approach.

What first attracted me to Community of Peace Academy was the emphasis on family and community. My work experience in family literacy has shown me the immense importance of parent involvement in a child's education. A family focus model encourages and empowers parents to become actively involved in their child's education and development. I strongly support Community of Peace Academy as a school that recognizes parents as a child's first teacher and is sensitive and committed to the partnership between home and school.

Community of Peace Academy is a special place. As a paraprofessional for two years, I always felt great pride to be part of such a professional, dedicated, optimistic and visionary team of educators. I would love to use my new education and skills to support the mission of Community of Peace Academy as an ESL teacher.

As I understand it, Community of Peace Academy places racial and cultural diversity, holism of human life, and a non violent prerogative as pillars of its vision and practice. I hold a conviction that the healing of

our complicated world will transpire if and only if we work collectively to create life affirming, socially conscious, and nurturing communities in which individuals derive self worth from their recognition and encouragement from the larger society, and at the same time, learn means to cultivate their own personal sanctuary of wholeness and well-being.

Kenneth Strike states, "It is of course to be earnestly desired that teachers be people of good character. I do not know how to reform the character of adult prospective teachers, and I am suspicious of those who believe they do. Getting people of good character should be treated as a problem of selection, not redemption" (1990, p. 208).

The new vision and philosophy we are exploring attract and inspire excellent staff members who are people of good character. Quality educators are eager for something to commit their lives to. That is why they enter the field of education in the first place, and too many are leaving public education too soon, because they do not find a noble purpose for staying. A schoolwide commitment to wholeness and fullness of life for all, when taken seriously and practiced faithfully, gives true meaning and purpose to our work and to our very lives.

Community of Peace Academy employs a diverse staff of nearly one hundred. They are women and men of all ages and of varying levels of experience. Some have previously lived or taught in foreign countries. They are African American, European American, Hmong, Hispanic, Lebanese, Eritrean, Chinese, Japanese, and Korean. They are gay and straight. They are men and women of varying faiths. Some do not actively practice any formal religious tradition.

The philosophy and mission upon which Community of Peace Academy was founded have appeal that transcends difference. It is universal in its appeal to the human condition and the human heart.

People who seriously commit themselves to being not only teachers and staff members, but role models, in a school with such a philosophy and mission, are good human beings. They are the kind of wise people that our children—all children—deserve.

On December 16, 2005, Chelle DeBarber, K–6 social worker at Community of Peace Academy, sent this unsolicited letter to all members of the staff. Chelle's poignant remarks are a tribute to the ethical and moral integrity of her colleagues.

Peace,

As I prepare for the Christmas season, I have thought about the gifts that Community of Peace staff give our students every day. I am reminded of a story that Leo Buscaglia, teacher, writer and lecturer, once shared. It reminds me of all of you.

Dr. Buscaglia traveled quite a bit. At Christmas time one year, he was traveling in Bali. He ended up staying in a small community during the holidays. He voiced his pleasure at being able to spend Christmas in such a beautiful place. The community was not Christian, and so did not know about Christmas. The young men asked him to explain. Dr. Buscaglia complied, telling them of the birth of Jesus. The young men thought it was a wonderful story, with the exception of one thing. They simply could not understand how no one would make room for Mary and Joseph, repeatedly asking, "How big were this Mary and this Joseph?" For you see, in their community there was always room for one more.

I am thankful for all the ways each of you make room. Not just in your classrooms, but in your hearts and minds, for our students. All students are accepted and loved here. I believe this is one of the greatest gifts we give our students. Because in love, we empower each student to be the best person they can be and to love others as well. I so appreciate all the little ways that you care for our students.

It is my sincere wish, that your holiday season be blessed with love and laughter and all the things you may need to be rejuvenated.

Deepest Regards,
Chelle

CHAPTER 11

Building on a Firm Foundation

Founding a charter school is like starting a small business. Some make it, and others do not. Within this very challenging environment, I have frequently been asked how it is that Community of Peace Academy has consistently achieved such success. This question has been posed to me with reference to, among other things, facilities, finances, governance, quality of staff, academics, and character education. Over the years, regardless of the topic of interest or who was asking, my answer has always been the same: Community of Peace Academy is successful because of an unwavering adherence to the vision, mission, and philosophy upon which it was founded.

Community of Peace Academy opened in 1995 with the intention of serving the most academically needy students in St. Paul, Minnesota—those who were traditionally on the wrong side of the achievement gap. Students enrolled at Community of Peace Academy that fall came from forty-one different schools and had the lowest test scores in the city. That first year, 78 percent were Hmong, recent immigrants from Laos and Thailand; 20 percent were African American or recent immigrants from Eritrea, a northern province of Ethiopia. Nearly 90 percent qualified for free or reduced-price lunch. The parents of these children were looking to us for answers.

On that first day of school in September of 1995, we were

grateful to be renting eight rooms, in a nearly vacant Catholic school building, to house 160 students in grades K–5. Our charter stated that we would add one grade each year, eventually serving grades K–8. When our fifth-grade students reached the eighth grade, their parents encouraged us to develop a high school. In 1998, our high school proposal was approved, and Community of Peace Academy High School became an unexpected reality.

In 1995, we could not have imagined that ten years later, we would have two impressive and functional additions to our facility, including a four-story high school, nor that we would be serving nearly six hundred students in grades K–12. We could not have imagined that in the year 2003, Community of Peace Academy would be one of ten schools in the United States to receive a National School of Character Award from the Character Education Partnership in Washington, D.C., the first charter school and the second Minnesota school to have been so honored. Nor could we have imagined, on our very first day, that in 2004, out of the nearly three thousand charter schools in America, the U.S. Department of Education's Office of Innovation and Improvement would select Community of Peace Academy as one of eight schools to feature in its publication titled *Successful Charter Schools*. According to then secretary of education, Rod Paige, "These schools were chosen after an exhaustive national search. They were primarily selected because they have demonstrated success, over time, in boosting student achievement."

Traditional public schools are under a great deal of pressure today. Never before have Americans been more critical of their public schools, and never before have they expected so much from them. With regard to chartered public schools, this pressure and criticism and these high expectations are greatly increased. Founding a charter school is like starting a small business. Some make it, and others do not. Within this very challenging environment, I have frequently been asked how it is that Community of Peace Academy has consistently achieved such success. This question has been posed to me with reference to, among other things, facilities, finances, governance, quality of staff, academics, and character education. Over the years, regardless of the topic of interest or who was asking, my answer has always been the same: Community of Peace Academy is successful because of an unwavering adherence to the vision, mission, and philosophy upon which it was founded.

The vision statement of Community of Peace Academy underlies the entire enterprise and is the bedrock upon which the school stands. It is both profoundly simple and profoundly complex:

> At Community of Peace Academy, our desired outcome is to educate the whole person—mind, body, and will—for peace, justice, freedom, compassion, wholeness and fullness of life for all.

This statement acknowledges that our students come to us whole. They are not only minds and bodies. They are also spiritual beings, each with free will, and what they decide, of their own free will, matters. It is not enough for America's public school graduates to be smart and strong. For their own sakes, and for the sake of others, they must also be good, and goodness is always the choice of a free will.

When the education of the free will, for moral goodness, becomes the bedrock of our organization, it profoundly impacts everything that is to follow. Every decision and action must support, with great integrity, this desired outcome. Achieving it demands a long-term commitment to personal moral excellence on the part of all members of the community.

> How do we create and sustain a moral learning community in a public school? How do we empower and inspire students to make life-giving decisions and choices for themselves and others? The mission statement and founding principles show the way.

MISSION STATEMENT

The mission of Community of Peace Academy is to be a racially and culturally diverse community of students, parents and staff, dedicated to creating a peaceful environment in which each person is treated with unconditional positive regard and acceptance. To create such an environment, a nonviolent perspective will be intentionally taught and all members of the community will strive to practice a nonviolent life style.

Within such an environment, each student will be empowered and inspired to reach his or her full potential academically, emotionally, physically and spiritually. Thus empowered and prepared, Community of Peace Academy students will commit themselves to meet the challenges posed by life in the multicultural world of the twenty-first century with confidence, compassion, intelligence, integrity and a positive regard for all.

FOUNDING PRINCIPLES

- Parents are the first educators of their children. Their relationship to the school must empower them to fulfill this primary role.

- Character development, based upon traditional concepts of respect, nonviolence, honesty, integrity, unselfishness, compassion, and self-discipline, should be the joint goal of home and school.

- Racial, ethnic and cultural diversity within our school community, expand our world-view and enrich our education.

- Respect and self-discipline are prerequisites to education, and are essential requirements in any learning community.

- Education happens in relationships, and thrives within a respectful, peaceful and value rich community.

- Members of the school staff play a significant role in building community by modeling positive values and caring, compassionate relationships with parents, colleagues and students.

- Respect for the environment, the earth and her inhabitants, the arts and the humanities are essential to a liberating education.

- Student academic achievement is the result of high expectations, empowerment, encouragement, guidance and hard work in addition to innate ability. Challenge and the promise of personal fulfillment will empower, strengthen and inspire our students.

Guided by these statements, Community of Peace Academy staff set out on their journey. To ensure that Community of Peace Academy would not violate the First Amendment in its efforts to teach ethical and moral behavior, only programs and curriculum of an ethical or moral nature that had been developed for public schools, and used in public schools elsewhere, were chosen.

The *Heartwood* ethics curriculum was adopted in our first year, in support of Thomas Groome's ontological pedagogy. This curriculum is organized around a group of beautifully written and illustrated multicultural folk and hero stories, legends, and contemporary tales and was developed by the Heartwood Institute in Pittsburgh, Pennsylvania. These excellent collections of children's literature were developed for grades K–6 and explore key character attributes common among the world's cultures: courage, loyalty, justice, respect, hope, honesty, and love.

These attributes are now deeply embedded within the culture of our K–12 school community. They are written on banners that hang on the walls of our gym—auditorium space. They are carried on banners in procession at the beginning of our most important community celebrations. One attribute is emphasized each month, and through the years we have made some adaptations and additions:

+ September: Peace
+ October: Caring and Respect
+ November: Thanksgiving and Gratitude
+ December: Honesty
+ January: Courage
+ February: Justice
+ March: Hope
+ April: Loyalty
+ May and June: Love

A quotation about the ethical principle of the month is featured at the top of the weekly staff bulletin, *Faculty Facts*. The monthly news bulletin, *Parent Talk*, features a reflection on the ethical principle of the month for parent and mentors. Examples of these publications follow.

⤚

FACULTY FACTS
MAY 22–26, 2006

LOVE: *Scientists are discovering at this very moment, that to live as if to live and love were one, is the only way of life for human beings, because, indeed, this is the way of life the innate nature of man demands.*

ASHLEY MONTAGU

MON., MAY 22

- Grade 8 Teachers will clean the Faculty Room this week. Thank you!
- Grades 4, 5, 6 Para's will clean the Faculty Work Room this week. Thank you!
- Ms. Molden's Girls will clean the cafeteria after breakfast this week. Thank you!
- 7:00 A.M., Facility Committee Meeting in HS Conference Room.
- 8:15 A.M., Hope Survey (Ms. Fischer's Advisory).
- 2:45–4:30 P.M., HS Spring Play Rehearsal in the Art Room.
- 2:50 P.M., HS Homework Club.
- 3:00 P.M., Baby Shower for Carrie Eicher in the K–8 Lounge.

TUES., MAY 23

- Happy Birthday to John Sorlien!
- Happy Birthday to Teresa Vazquez de Nilsson!
- 8:15 A.M., Hope Survey (Ms. Zosel's Advisory).
- 12:45–2:15 P.M., Third Grade Drama Residency. Mu Performing Arts.
- 2:45–4:00 P.M., Choralier's Rehearsal in the music room.
- 2:45–3:45 P.M., Hip Hop Club potluck party in the art room.
- 2:45–4:00 P.M., Science Club in Ms. Kersting's room.
- 2:50 P.M., HS Homework Club.
- 2:40–5:00 P.M., Chess Club in Mr. Ghebregzi's room for Grades 7/12.

+ 2:50 P.M., Grades 7/8 Team Meeting.
+ 3:00 P.M., Peace/Ethics Committee. Ms. Sanchez's room.
+ 3:00 P.M., Staff Development Committee in K–8 Lounge.
+ 6:00–8:00 P.M., SPED Advisory Council Parent Information Meeting. Art Room.

WED., MAY 24

+ Planning Day for Grades 3 and 4 Teachers.
+ 8:30–Noon, Grade 1 to Raptor Center at Como Park.
+ 2:50 P.M., Grades 7/8 Homework Club.
+ 8:15 A.M., Hope Survey (Mr. Acker's Advisory).
+ 2:45–4:30 P.M., HS Spring Play Rehearsal in the Art Room.
+ 2:50 P.M., HS Homework Club.
+ 2:40 P.M., HS Student Council in Mr. Acker's Room.
+ 2:50–4:00 P.M., Framework for Teaching Task Force. Annual Review. K-8 Lounge.
+ 3:00 P.M., K–6 Picnic Planning Team Meeting in Ms. Molden's room.
+ 3:00 P.M., HS Science Club to visit Body Works Exhibit at MN Science Museum.

THURS., MAY 25

+ Happy Birthday to Tang Thao! Grades 7/8 Para.
+ Annual Meeting/Spring Sing Rehearsals throughout the day. See Schedule, May 21 e-mail.
+ 1:15 P.M., Junior Great Books for Grade 4 Students.
+ 12:45–2:15 P.M., Third Grade Drama Residency. Mu Performing Arts.
+ 8:15 A.M., Hope Survey (Ms. Kersting's Advisory).
+ 2:45–4:30 P.M., HS Spring Play Rehearsal in the Art Room.
+ 2:50–4:30 P.M., HS Guitar Club.
+ 2:50–3:50 P.M., HS Team Meeting.
+ 6:30–8:00 P.M., Community of Peace Academy Annual Meeting and Spring Program.

FRI., MAY 26

- Happy Birthday to Carrie Eicher!
- Happy Birthday to Kao Lee Xiong! Kindergarten Para.
- Happy Birthday to Lou Trudeau and Paul Schettner! Their birthdays are on Sunday, May 28.
- 8:20 A.M.–2:15 P.M., Grade 2 to MN Zoo, Exploring Animals.
- 8:30 A.M., K–8 Recycling today. Thank you fourth graders!
- 9:15 A.M., Grades 7/8 Student Council meeting in HS conference room.
- 10:30–11:15 A.M., High school drama class performance in the art room.
- 12:45–2:20 P.M., 6A and 6B to Arlington Library.
- 8:15 A.M., Hope Survey (Mr. Fleming's Advisory).

Parent Talk

December, 2005

Dear Parent/Mentors,

I recently heard a story that was told by Felix, an eighty year old man from Sri Lanka who was in St. Paul visiting a friend of mine. In 1955, Felix made his first trip from Sri Lanka to the Twin Cities. He was a young pastor and was being prepared to visit a church in a small town in South Dakota. The person who was preparing him, told him that if the Indians asked him for money, he was not to give them any. The person instructing him, assured him that the people of South Dakota, "took good care of the Indians." Felix thought this was interesting advice and he remembered it.

The next day, he boarded a bus and began his travels from St. Paul to South Dakota. On the bus, he noticed a man who looked like he might be an Indian. The man also noticed Felix and kept looking at him. Felix began to think about what the person had told him. He thought about what he would do when the man asked him for money and he tried to decide how much money might be the right amount to give. Soon, the Indian came and sat with him and they began to talk. The bus stopped at every town along the way and so they had a good long visit. The time came when the Indian got out his wallet. Felix thought, "Well here it comes. Now he will surely ask me for money." However, much to his surprise, the Indian took out a worn dollar bill and gave it to Felix. Felix tried to give back the gift and told the man that he did not need money. The Indian insisted that he keep the dollar bill. He told Felix, "You are in America now. A day will come when you are hungry and in need of food, and no one will help you." To this day, Felix carries that dollar bill as a reminder of the truth.

Our ethical principle for the month of December is HONESTY. At Community of Peace Academy, we recite the PeaceBuilder's Pledge. From kindergarten to the twelfth grade, students are taught, among other things, to Seek Wise People. What is honesty? What does it mean to be a wise person? Honesty is the ability to tell the truth. We can only tell the truth, if we know what the truth is. A wise person, is one who seeks the truth. This is a life long search. When we close our minds and hearts to others, we may miss the truth.

Our children are looking to us for truth. We are their wise people. This is a great responsibility. May we keep our minds, our eyes and our hearts open to truth, especially to the truth of our sisters and brothers who are racially or culturally different than ourselves. This is the way to Wisdom. This is the way to Peace.

Peace to you and to your dear children,

Dr. Rusthoven

Growing Communities for Peace, a conflict resolution program for young children, was also adopted in our first year. Having been developed locally by Julie Peterson and Rebecca Janke, this program contained many of the elements we had proposed for our charter school. Teachers were taught how to conduct daily Peace Circles. The program introduced the use of Talking Sticks. To ensure that each person would be heard, the Talking Stick was passed around the circle. When you held the stick, you had the floor and others were taught to listen respectfully. Each room would have a Peace Table where children would go to settle conflicts. A Peace Maker Puppet was used to teach conflict resolution skills. This program proved helpful and was especially effective for the primary grades. However, it soon became apparent that for our older students, more was needed.

Research led us to Heartsprings, Inc. (now PeacePartners, Inc.), and the *PeaceBuilders* program. Dr. Dennis Enbry had developed this program in Tucson, Arizona, for students in grades K–6, and in 2000, it was expanded to include grades 7 and 8. The PeaceBuilders program is research based and focuses upon a set of conflict prevention principles. These principles are taught and practiced throughout the school and are included in the PeaceBuilders Pledge, which is recited daily in each classroom:

> *I am a PeaceBuilder.*
> *I pledge to Praise People,*
> *To Give Up Putdowns,*
> *To Seek Wise People,*
> *To Notice and Speak Up About Hurts I Have Caused,*
> *To Right Wrongs,*
> *And to Help Others.*
> *I will build peace at home, at school*
> *and in my community each day.*

In her junior year at Community of Peace Academy, Keonna Brown wrote the following essay, describing how the PeaceBuilders Pledge has influenced her life:

The PeaceBuilders Pledge was taught to me when I started first grade in 1995. Back then, it was just a part of the day, like gym or lunch, nothing to really make a big deal about. Now, not only is it still part of the day, but it is also a piece of my life. Even with all the violence going on in the world around me, I can still wake up each day with a smile. Not because I am pleased with what's going on, but because I know that this is just another day for me to make a difference.

Going to Community of Peace Academy, I have learned that there really are peaceful ways of solving problems. I have also learned that these ways are more efficient and more effective. Once I really started to understand the PeaceBuilders Pledge, I also started to understand myself. Ever since I decided to live peacefully, I became less stressed out, my grades turned around and I became a lot happier.

Peace builders are similar to the domino effect. When one person decides to either stand up for his or herself, or even for someone else, it inspires others to do the same. Or if they decide not to make fun of someone, others will follow. Peace builders are the ones making the differences every day. They are the heroes.

There is nothing like living peacefully. It's a sort of a feeling that you get when everything is going wrong, yet you don't panic, because you know everything will be ok. It's the power of the peace builder.

～

The Community of Peace Academy Code of Caring Behaviors, referenced in chapter 8, and the principles set forth in the PeaceBuilders Pledge have become the foundation of the discipline policies and procedures at the grade school. Following violations, K–8 students are invited to reflect upon the Code of Caring Behaviors and the PeaceBuilders Pledge and to tell which parts they forgot and what they might do differently in the future. In this way these documents have become part of our common language and are deeply imbedded in the school culture beginning in kindergarten and continuing through the end of high school.

Each August, at a staff retreat held on the first staff day of the school year, the entire K–12 staff is invited to sign the PeaceBuilders School Commitment Pledge, thus pledging their individual support to uphold the principles of this program. All staff members are also invited to complete a PeaceBuilder Wise Person form. These forms, which are displayed in the hallway outside the business office, include a picture and interesting information introducing each Wise Person to the students, and to all community members.

Students and staff are taught and encouraged to write meaningful Praise Notes to others, expressing praise for specific qualities of character or kindnesses. Putdowns are discouraged and are no longer a part of the prevailing culture of Community of Peace Academy. Both students and staff can often be heard reminding one another with a smile, "That was a putdown," or, "You are not being a peace builder." During home visits, families are given a copy of the PeaceBuilders Pledge to post on their refrigerator, and parents often report that students use PeaceBuilders language at home, just as they do at school. In 2005, PeacePartners, Inc., named Community of Peace Academy one of eight Model PeaceBuilders Sites (out of six hundred PeaceBuilders Schools).

In our third year, one of our teachers heard of the *Responsive Classroom* program from a colleague who was teaching sixth grade in a traditional public school nearby. She went to visit, was sincerely impressed by what she observed, and attended a week of training to learn Responsive Classroom techniques. Her enthusiasm for this excellent program was contagious, and soon our seventh-grade teacher also chose to attend the training. As more teachers began to request Responsive Classroom training, it was decided that we would bring the trainers to Community of Peace

Academy and offer the program to our entire staff. Today, every teacher in grades K–8 has received this training, and ongoing coaching is provided.

Responsive Classroom was developed over a decade ago by the Northeast Foundation for Children (NEFC), located in Greenfield, Massachusetts. The program promotes the development of a social curriculum in public elementary classrooms, grades K–8, and is now made available by Origins, which is located in Minneapolis, Minnesota. The NEFC mission is to help teachers see their academic instruction and curriculum content in a broader and more encompassing context of social interaction and moral purpose for their students. Written by Ruth Sidney-Charney, NEFC cofounder, the book *Teaching Children to Care: Management in the Responsive Classroom* has had a significant influence on classroom practice and teacher training.

The Responsive Classroom is built around six central components that integrate teaching, learning, and caring in the daily program. Based upon the Golden Rule, the components are set in the context of commonly shared values, such as honesty, fairness, and respect:

+ Classroom Organization that provides active interest areas for students, space for student-centered displays of work, and an appropriate mix of whole class, group, and individual instruction.

+ Morning Meeting format that provides children the daily opportunity to practice greetings, conversation, sharing, and problem solving, and motivates them to meet academic challenges of the day ahead. Morning meeting greatly strengthened our original Peace Circles.

+ Rules and Logical Consequences that are generated, modeled, and role-played with the children and that become the cornerstone of classroom life.

+ Academic Choice for all children each day in which they must take control of their own learning in some meaningful way, both individually and cooperatively.

+ Guided Discovery of learning materials, areas of the room, curriculum content, and ways of behaving that moves children through a deliberate and careful introduction to each new experience. It is not assumed that children already know how to do something before they begin.

+ Assessment and Reporting to parents that is an evolving process of mutual communication and understanding.

When put into practice, the Responsive Classroom has great potential for educating the free human will for moral goodness.

When the high school was founded, it presented new challenges. All of the curriculum and programs we had previously used to teach ethics and peace had been developed for grades K–8. Yet, as Keonna Brown's essay demonstrates, the impact of Heartwood, PeaceBuilders, and Responsive Classroom carried over into the high school. The Heartwood ethical principles were universal and were now a part of our community. PeaceBuilders conflict prevention principles were solid and provided moral guidance for all of us, students and adults. They were not directly taught at the high school, but their influence continued. A Peace Pledge was developed for the high school. However, at community gatherings, the original Peace Pledge is still used. The high school peace pledge follows:

> Peace begins with me. Therefore, I pledge:
> to encourage people,
> to give up put downs,
> to seek wise people as advisors and friends,

to take responsibility for hurts I cause
to right wrongs,
and to help others.
Today I will choose peace,
and I will share my peace with others.

The first program introduced specifically at the secondary level was *Project Wisdom*. Developed in Houston, Texas, the objectives of this grades 7–12 program are as follows:

+ To encourage students to take responsibility for their choices and actions.

+ To place role models before students by quoting individuals who have contributed to humanity.

+ To teach tolerance and understanding of different races, cultures, and religions.

+ To encourage students to think by asking them questions that require reflection and inner searching.

+ To counteract the negativity in the world with positive thoughts and ideas.

Each morning during high school announcements, a student reads one quote and the brief reflection that accompanies it. Teachers may build upon this by encouraging students to journal and/or to discuss it further in the classroom. Materials are available to guide this process.

From the beginning, the high school schedule has included ethics. Currently, the high school day begins with a forty-five-minute Ethics/Advisory period. All teachers teach ethics to the students they advise and act as advisors for the same group of students for two years.

The Responsive Classroom practice of conducting Morning

Meetings was adapted and continued at the high school. These classroom meetings were called Ethics Circles and were held during Advisory. Through the years, some of the high school teachers have attended Responsive Classroom Middle School Training and adapted it to their students' needs. During the summer of 2006, Community of Peace Academy high school staff enthusiastically agreed to participate in the first Responsive Classroom training offered specifically for high school teachers. It is our hope that Responsive Classroom training regarding Morning Meetings will strengthen the high school Ethics Circles, and assist in building trust and caring relationships with and among students.

The high school staff have developed distinct Ethics courses for each grade level around the following topics:

+ Grade 9: Personal Ethics: Care for Self/Care for Learning

+ Grade 10: Personal Ethics: Care for Others/Care for the Environment

+ Grade 11: World Religions

+ Grade 12: World Peace Makers

In addition to the daily Ethics period, a monthly Ethics Forum features invited guests who share their own stories and/or speak on ethical topics or issues. Among those who have visited are the following:

+ Carl Eller, Minnesota Vikings Hall of Fame: *Being a winner in our personal lives as well as in our professional lives.*

+ Jane Ramseyer-Miller, director of One Voice GLBT (Gay, Lesbian, Bisexual, Transgender) Mixed Chorus, and John Sorlien, director of the Academy Choir: *Coming Out and Coming Together: A GLBT Perspective.* This presentation preceded a collaboration between One Voice Mixed Chorus and the Academy Choir that included the premiere of a piece of music especially commissioned for the program and ended with a thrilling joint concert, *Building Bridges.*

+ Nellie Trocme Hewett: *How the weapons of the spirit can counter even organized prejudice carried out by powerful nations in wartime.*

+ Joe Carter: *The power of music to express and heal the wounds of history.*

+ Hector Garcia: *Mexican-born businessman and activist in Minnesota, on finding your real person and living up to your full potential.*

+ Catherine Guisan, Ph.D.: *European integration since the Second World War as a project for peace in a region known for its wars.*

+ Minnesota State Senator Mee Moua: *Her personal story as the first Hmong woman to become a state senator.*

+ Bobby Brown: *Victim of a random gang shooting, Bobby has overcome a debilitating injury and has become a role model for youth through spiritual strength and determination.*

+ Dr. Blong Xiong: *Dr. Xiong arrived in America at the age of fifteen with two years of formal education. He overcame tremendous odds to become one of the first Hmong immigrants to earn a Ph.D. from the University of Minnesota.*

At Community of Peace Academy, service to others is encouraged at all grades. Students take turns wiping tables and sweeping floors in the cafeteria after breakfast and lunch each day. Each year, each class plans a service project. During the 2006–2007 school year, a service-learning program is being introduced at the high school. When the program is fully developed, ninth-grade students will spend one afternoon each week volunteering in the community.

Every fall since 2001, the eleventh-grade class has participated in a two-week Habitat for Humanity project. This has become a cherished experience for our students. Originally sponsored by the House of Hope Presbyterian Church, in St. Paul, Community of Peace Academy students are now sponsored directly by Habitat for Humanity. The organization truly values their good work and the diversity that their participation brings. Many adult volunteers are needed each year to support the students on the work sites. Following are portions of a letter received from Dave Healy, one of our Habitat for Humanity adult volunteers, fall of 2004:

> I congratulate you and your colleagues at CPA for the obvious success of your commitment to character education. The students I worked with yesterday consistently impressed me with their dedication, spirit and resolve. They worked hard, followed directions, and entered into the tasks at hand with humor, patience, and good will. In short, they were a pleasure to work with.
>
> We live in a time that emphasizes testing in schools. It will continue to be important for CPA students to perform well on various academic tests. However, the best test of what a school is doing occurs when its students move outside school walls and into the surrounding community---the arena where the fruits of their education will be displayed. From what I observed yesterday, CPA's teachers and staff can be extremely proud of your students and their preparedness to make a difference in the world.

Community of Peace Academy contracts with Youth Frontiers, Inc., to provide a series of assemblies and retreats for students and staff. Founded in 1987, the mission of this organization is "To change the way young people treat each other in every hallway, lunch-line and classroom of every school in America." During the 2005–2006 school year, Youth Frontiers activities included a Kindness Assembly for third and fourth grade, Kindness Retreat for fifth grade, Courage Retreat for seventh and eighth grade, and Respect Retreat for ninth grade. These proved to be engaging and meaningful experiences and will continue into the future. Youth Frontiers also offered an Honor Retreat for the Community of Peace Academy staff in August of 2006.

As was previously mentioned, Community of Peace Academy was named a National School of Character in 2003, by the Character Education Partnership in Washington, D.C. The Character Education Partnership offers Eleven Principles of Effective Character Education, developed by Tom Lickona, Eric Schaps, and Catherine Lewis. While Lickona and his colleagues state that there is no single script for effective character education, they have devised these principles as a guide to schools and groups in planning a character education effort and/or to evaluate available character education programs, books, and resources:

1. Character education promotes core ethical values as the basis of good character.

2. "Character" must be comprehensively defined to include thinking, feeling, and behavior.

3. Effective character education requires an intentional, proactive, and comprehensive approach that promotes the core values in all phases of school life.

4. The school must be a caring community.

5. To develop character, students need opportunities for moral action.

6. Effective character education includes a meaningful and challenging academic curriculum that respects all learners and helps them succeed.

7. Character education should strive to develop students' intrinsic motivation.

8. The school staff must become a learning and moral community in which all share responsibility for character education and attempt to adhere to the same core values that guide the education of students.

9. Character education requires moral leadership from staff and students.

10. The school must recruit parents and community members as full partners in the character-building effort.

11. Evaluation of character education should assess the character of the school, the school staff's functioning as character educators, and the extent to which students manifest good character.

These eleven principles illustrate that character education is a complex undertaking. It is a way of life, which must be clearly articulated and practiced by everyone. Young people learn about the moral values of a community, not so much by reading and studying about them as by watching and experiencing them in action. Therefore, it is of critical importance that adult members of the community willingly embrace and model in their own lives the ethical and moral values that they hope to teach. At Community of Peace Academy, such an expectation appears on teachers' contracts. Still, mandating this commitment will not make it so.

Relationships are a key factor in the equation. Structuring the school so as to promote a rich sense of community and caring relationships among all its members is essential. Like most Catholic schools, Community of Peace Academy is a small learning community that serves a wide grade span, grades K to 12, thus promoting trusting, caring, supportive relationships among all members of the school community—parents, staff, and students—*over time*. Additionally, time is intentionally set aside each day in each classroom for the important process of strengthening relationships and building community. Morning Meetings and Ethics Circles greatly enhance this process.

Community of Peace Academy's results on the 2004 Minnesota Student Survey bear witness to the positive impact of these combined efforts; even more so when differences in state and Community of Peace Academy demographics are taken into consideration. Although students in both grades 9 and 12 were tested, only the ninth-grade results were published, due to the small size of the class of 2004 and concerns regarding confidentiality.

Feelings about School

+ 60 percent of our ninth graders like school very much or quite a bit versus 56 percent statewide.

Perceptions of School Environment

+ 57 percent of our ninth graders said that all or most of the students in school are friendly versus 57 percent statewide.

+ 71 percent of our ninth graders said a few or none of the students in school have made fun of them or threatened students of different races or backgrounds versus 58 percent statewide.

+ 78 percent of our ninth graders said that all or most of their teachers are interested in them as people versus 36 percent statewide.

Perceptions of School Safety

+ 95 percent of our ninth graders strongly agree that they feel safe going to and from school versus 94 percent statewide.

+ 94 percent of our ninth graders strongly agree or agree that they feel safe at school versus 90 percent statewide.

+ 39 percent of our ninth graders strongly *disagree* that student use of alcohol or drugs is a problem at this school versus 8 percent statewide.

Victimization at School

+ 30 percent of our ninth graders have been insulted on school property versus 62 percent statewide.

+ 5 percent of our ninth graders have been threatened on school property versus 27 percent statewide.

+ 32 percent of our ninth graders have been pushed, shoved, or grabbed on school property versus 45 percent statewide.

At Community of Peace Academy, collaboration and positive relationships among members of the staff are encouraged by providing team planning days once each month. Members of the staff need time to socialize. They deserve to be treated well and with kindness. Staff events and celebrations include an August Retreat that focuses upon each person's inner peace; a breakfast in late August, at which new staff members are introduced and welcomed; an annual Hmong Culture Dinner, prepared by parents, at which staff members new to the school are introduced to and celebrate the Hmong culture with their colleagues; a winter holiday gathering; an annual staff appreciation breakfast; and an end-of-year celebration where those leaving our community are acknowledged. In addition to these special events, dinner is served for teachers before evening conferences, and meetings are enhanced by refreshments and often begin with time to socialize.

Relationships among staff members are caring and respectful, and members of the staff are generous in expressing their encouragement, appreciation, and support for one another. The following e-mail, sent to the high school assistant principal (Tim McGowan) and social worker (Molly Heisenfelt) from a member of the elementary special education team, is an example of this:

Dear Tim and Molly,

I just wanted you to know what I experienced yesterday and today. Yesterday, as I walked out of the building at the end of the day I was carrying an empty two-drawer file cabinet that I brought in from home and decided to take out again as it wasn't needed, I was warmly greeted by Tom and Jordan who stopped their conversation to greet me and hold open the door. Jordan asked if I needed help and I said yes and he picked-up and hauled the cabinet to my car. On the way to the car we had a brief, but meaningful conversation about his life. He shared he's going through a rough time with something at home, etc. As an adult child of an alcoholic, I was able to share that for me, things got better, and I hope they will for him too. Anyway, it was the kind of conversation that showed connection and trust and a sense that this kid felt he mattered to me even though I have had very limited time with him and don't work in the high school. I was so touched by how both Jordan and Tom treated me. Today, I stayed home half a day as I am battling a cold. As I walked up to the building juggling my things, Rose Marie held the door open for me and gave a warm greeting. At other schools I've had the experience of walking in and out of junior highs and high schools and someone like me would be largely invisible or ignored by kids. Worse, I have walked in and out of doors where I felt negative energy, even scorn from kids. These CPA kids are soooooooo different, they showed genuine human connection and good will. Something good must be happening in that high school!!!

Sincerely,
Shirley Klitzke

At Community of Peace Academy, it is a foundational belief that everyone in the community is of equal value and that each person deserves to be treated with unconditional positive regard. This is an extremely important and powerful concept and an essential component in assuring collaboration and positive human relationships.

Unconditional positive regard for all requires humility from all. It requires the willingness to forgive—not only large offenses, but small, everyday annoyances that are not meant to offend. It is a *love principle* and a prerequisite for living in true community. It is achieved when all members of the community strive for I–Thou relationships.

When this powerful principle is put into practice, things such as position, economic status, age, sex, race, culture, disability, and sexual orientation no longer determine how we will treat others or who will be treated well. Our positive regard has no such conditions. To the extent that any person or organization practices this principle, they will experience tremendous benefits. Amazingly, it brings out the best in everyone. When every person in the organization is shown equal regard and appreciation, each one is likely to give, in return, the very best he or she has to offer.

When visiting Community of Peace Academy, people often comment on the attractive appearance of our facilities. We have an amazing crew of custodians who keep our building not only clean and in good repair but sparkling. Recently, our cafeteria supervisor shared a story with me. She shared it because she was inspired by it. On the day of high school graduation, one of our custodians was cleaning the cafeteria floor. He was not just cleaning it, he was making it shine. The cafeteria supervisor noted this and told him how beautiful it looked. He stopped his work and replied to her, with great feeling, "My friends are graduating tonight. All their families and friends will be here. I want it to look beautiful for them!"

A school or organization can never be all that it could be without the combined best efforts of each person. Every person deserves unconditional positive regard, because every person in the school community truly is of equal value. Every person's contribution is essential. When each person within an organization is striving to practice this principle, as well as reaping its benefits, the outcome is awesome! Most important, when children experience the impact of being treated with unconditional positive regard day after day, they learn to believe unconditionally in their own enormous potential.

Within a moral learning community, it is imperative that parents are treated with unconditional positive regard and that they are honored as their children's first and primary educators and respected as equal partners in the education process. This was perhaps one of the things that most impressed me about the Catholic schools in which I worked. The administrators and teachers seemed to have no particular regard for race, creed, or economic status. Each parent was treated with equal esteem. This has a powerful effect upon children. Cummins (1986) was right. You cannot inspire a child to reach his or her full potential if the child knows that you do not esteem his or her parents, and children always know.

At Community of Peace Academy, parents are invited to attend fall registration nights in August, thus providing an opportunity to meet teachers before the school year begins. To strengthen relationships with families, home visits are made to each home each year. These are scheduled at fall registration and are conducted after school hours during September and October. As most families have several children, teachers usually visit in pairs. Interpreters and ESL teachers often participate as well. A Home Visit Check List is provided. Among other things, parents are encouraged to share their hopes and dreams for their child. These become a part of the students' annual academic, personal, and peace builder/spiritual goals. These goals are reviewed with parents at conferences held later in the school year.

Home visits provide a level of understanding that is not attainable in any other way. Upon visiting the home of one of her students, the teacher found that the family had no chairs. Suddenly, she understood why the child had such difficulty sitting on her chair during lessons! Although the visits are taxing, teachers routinely express their appreciation of them. Those who have taught at the school for many years especially enjoy seeing siblings of current students who were their former students. In such cases, the visits take on new and unexpected levels of meaning.

Parents are invited to school each month for a Parent Night, performance, or conference. Annual Parent Nights include a focus on Peace Education in January, a Multicultural Family Event in February, and Turn Off the TV Night in April. In addition to these topics, parent education is offered. For example, during the 2005–2006 school year, Dr. Blong Xiong from the University of Minnesota presented four sessions on child development and the importance of education, one session each in English and Spanish and two in Hmong. Transportation, child care, and interpreters are provided as needed. It is customary that 95 percent to 100 percent of parents attend K–8 conferences, and 75 percent to 80 percent attend conferences at the high school.

Parents who are stressed by economic and social issues need our attention and support, and they often need our patient understanding as well. Many are new immigrants, teen parents, single parents, or parents struggling with various addictions. When they fail to meet our expectations, they need forgiveness and the reassurance that we still believe in them and respect them. Even under favorable circumstances, most parents long to be part of a stable and supportive community, a community whose values will assist them in raising their children. Schools that are moral learning communities can provide guidance and support over time that have the potential to change not only students' but also parents' lives for the better.

At the conclusion of our winter program, one of our parents and her two daughters, then in grades 8 and 9, came forward carrying a large package. Their joy was evident as they invited me to join them. The family had been part of our community for ten years. For as long as we had known the girls, their mother had struggled with addiction issues. Since the girls were in first and second grades, the school had been an anchor for this family. With tears in her eyes, the mother thanked me for Community of Peace Academy and for the support that she and her family had received. Then she presented me with a beautiful afghan that *she* had made for *me*. It will always remain a cherished gift. I am not only the principal and she a struggling parent: we are equal members of a moral learning community. I have learned much from her, and, hopefully, she has learned much from me.

Since 1995, Community of Peace Academy has implemented, with great success, a multitude of programs and initiatives that have potential to empower and inspire students to make life-giving decisions and choices. Yet there are no guarantees. This is challenging work and requires the total commitment of each member of the community each and every day.

On Thursday, October 27, 2005, over ten years of devotion to the education of the whole person for fullness of life for all was put to the test. On that day, a loud verbal fight broke out between three girls in the cafeteria during the high school lunch period. This rare occurrence immediately drew the attention of everyone, and friends of the combatants quickly rushed in to separate them.

One was taken to the office of the cafeteria supervisor, one was sent to the high school office, and I set out to find the other girl, who, I had been told, was heading toward the hallway. I found her there, quietly talking to her boyfriend. I calmly asked him to return to class and told her that she would need to follow me to the grade school office, where I set about the task of calling parents to come and pick up their daughters until meetings could be arranged.

I would soon hear the news that as he walked through the cafeteria on his way back to class, the student's boyfriend made a statement that he had a gun and would shoot people after school. A student whose friend was on the other side of the argument overheard him talking. The student immediately reported the threat to Tim McGowan. Immediately, Tim went to find the boy and brought him into his office, where he and Molly Heisenfelt questioned him. The boy was cooperative and admitted that he had made the statement about the gun and his intention to use it. The three then quietly proceeded to the boy's locker where nothing was found, and then to his car. A sawed-off shotgun was found in the back of the car. Just before afternoon dismissal, the boy was taken into police custody.

On January 31, 2006, headlines on the front page of the *St. Paul Pioneer Press* reported, "39 knew of Red Lake killer's plan." We will never know if the Community of Peace Academy student who was taken into police custody that day would have acted upon his threat. The human will is a great mystery. What we do know is that factors that had been intentionally put into place, over a period of nearly eleven consecutive years, worked together to ensure a peaceful ending on that particular day.

Although we cannot say, with absolute assurance, what led to this ending, we are grateful for the fact that a student took the threat seriously and felt safe enough within the school community to report it. The police were amazed by the calm relationships that existed between the perpetrator and Mr. McGowan and Ms.

Heisenfelt, and stated that on a safety scale of 1 to 10, they would give the school a 10.

As public educators, our challenge is clear. We must acknowledge the power of free will for good or for evil. The threat of violence is real and pervasive. Keeping violence at bay requires constant attention to the human spirit and to the moral climate of the school. This is our best hope. Peace begins with us.

CHAPTER 12

Where Peace Begins

Children deserve teachers who are hopeful, positive people. Spiritually healthy adults inspire the spirits of their students and give them a vision of lives that are whole and full.

If you have traveled by air, you have heard this admonition: "Please secure your own oxygen mask before attempting to assist others." Likewise, we cannot foster emotional and spiritual wholeness in the lives of our students if we are not, on most days, emotionally and spiritually whole.

When I was an urban Catholic school principal, I looked for three qualities when hiring staff: solid academic preparation in their chosen field, demonstrated interest and experience working in diverse settings, and a commitment to their own spiritual growth. Potential candidates who were found lacking in any category would not be hired.

As I contemplated the hiring process for Community of Peace Academy, it was evident that these same three qualities would be essential in our employees. I was not sure how to approach the spiritual component. In truth, I was not concerned about the religious affiliation of a perspective candidate. Over the years, I had developed a very broad understanding of spirituality. However, if our vision was to educate the whole person—if we were committed to helping students reach their full potential, not only academically and physically, but also emotionally and spiritually—then our staff would need be invested in their own wholeness. They would need to be aware of, and invested in, their own spiritual health and well-being.

Special attention was given to the interview process. Questions focused on the candidate as a whole person and on all aspects of the school. Of all of the interview questions, this one has seemed to hold the key to finding educators who understand the concept of wholeness and fullness of life for all:

> The mission statement of Community of Peace Academy states that each student will be empowered and inspired to reach his or her full potential, academically, emotionally, physically, and spiritually. We adults must be their role models. With this in mind, how do you care for your own academic, emotional, physical and spiritual growth, and well-being and please speak to each area.

This question is greeted by various reactions. Candidates often respond, "Wow, that's a good question. No one has ever asked me a question like that before!" If a candidate truly does not understand the spiritual part of this question, the chances are that he or she would soon become overwhelmed and discouraged. Adults who are not spiritually healthy, when faced with the daily realities and challenges of urban education, often become cynical, pessimistic, impatient, unforgiving of others, and negative. A former Community of Peace Academy teacher expressed it this way:

> *Basically, if you're teaching urban education, it can be such a hopeless task that you'd better have your spiritual house in order or it will kill you. And I look at teachers from other urban schools who are walking zombies all the time and I can't . . . I don't want to become a walking zombie. There are*

many, many, many teachers who are just putting in their time because they feel that they are too invested in the pension and they can't see any other way of life, although they should be doing something else very definitely. This is a very, very hard job and you do need to be spiritually centered or it will . . . it doesn't kill you physically . . . and I've seen a number of people become very physically ill over it . . . it will kill your spirit.

Children deserve teachers who are hopeful, positive people. Spiritually healthy adults inspire the spirits of their students and give them a vision of lives that are whole and full.

At Community of Peace Academy, first and foremost, teachers' contracts state that they will strive to understand and model the mission and philosophy of the school. All members of the staff are asked to set annual professional, personal, and spiritual goals. Spiritual goals vary widely. Spiritual wholeness means different things to different people.

Here are some examples of the spiritual goals of members of the Community of Peace Academy staff:

To be more appreciative of my life on a daily basis and stay away from negative perceptions of myself, my life, and those around me.

Reflect on experiences in my life through journaling.

Become involved in our church community.

Be more confident in the choices I make.

Schedule and keep sacred a time for daily prayer.

Read daily meditations and continue to write in my journal/ reflect.

I would like to take a weekend retreat by myself, probably to Chicago.

Attend my small group Bible study every Thursday night (except school Board nights).

I'm currently reading more about Islam and Buddhism. My goal is to better understand what these faiths stand for.

Pray, go to church more often. More communication with people.

Reconnect with friends, especially with close friends who are physically distant.

Have conversations with mentors about growth they see in me and goals I need to set.

Finish my reading of the New Testament before September 2005.

Continue to ask forgiveness, guidance and strength daily.

I will continue with my quiet time in the morning. It's the only way I survive. It calms me so I can be my best.

To search for truth both inside and outside the realm of Islamic and Judeo Christian morality, through "doubt" rather than "faith."

To set aside at least 1/2 hour each day for myself (workout or even nap).

To have a stronger walk with God.

Remain active in politics. Continue to work for positive change.

I would like to connect myself with God more. I need to learn he comes before all else and not only know it, but truly and wholeheartedly believe it.

I'd like to find ways of being more supportive of my colleagues. Many people have been very generous to me. I'd really like to give back consistently and freely.

Weekly regular mass attendance.

Volunteer at least once a month to help people in need.

To give thanks in good AND bad times for the life that I have been given, and to let God guide me toward consistently seeing the positive things in life.

Spend time praying with other Christians (women) at work.

We have recently started memorizing Scripture as a family. I would like to set as a goal continuing to do that together throughout the next year.

I would like to find a new church or congregation to join. I moved.

I will continue to make music and grow musically.

To put my faith in God and trust in his plan for me, without questioning so much.

Take time every day for meditation and reflection to help me be calm and understanding toward others.

To experience the effectiveness of silence as a discipline in deepening my relationship to God.

Listen more fully—to others, to my inner voice, to elders—and continue to act for social justice.

Teaching in a school challenged daily by the effects of poverty, and by the realities of our prevailing culture, is hard work indeed. Sustaining the required effort over time requires great spiritual and emotional strength. Schools that are serious about leaving no child behind would be wise to take note of this. Teachers and staff members in public schools benefit as greatly as their students do when wholeness and fullness of life are the desired outcomes for all.

A frequent volunteer at Community of Peace Academy once remarked that the school seems to be "enchanted." I assured her that it may appear to be enchanted but that the culture of the school was actually the result of a deep commitment on the part of each one of us. To the extent that each and every member of the staff comes to work each and every day, spiritually centered, at peace within, and committed to sharing peace with others—to that extent, that day, our school will be a community of peace. It happens one person, one human interaction at a time. A true commitment to the principles upon which Community of Peace Academy is founded changes everything. Thus we prepare the fertile soil in which teaching and learning are transformed.

CHAPTER 13

Transforming Teaching and Learning

What most often sabotages the efforts of public school reformers is lack of attention to human relationships within the school. The new vision I am proposing for America's public schools creates the conditions for positive, sustained transformation of public education. Being given the autonomy to follow such a vision, and fully embracing and implementing it, unleashes amazing potential.

In 1991, Minnesota passed the first charter school law in America, offering chartered public schools autonomy in exchange for results. The autonomy provided to charter schools through this legislation is our best hope, to date, for real reform of public education in America. It is this autonomy that allows us the freedom to explore various philosophies and to give them time to take root, to flourish and to bear fruit. Of equal importance, charter schools, at their best, put decision-making authority squarely in the hands of those closest to students: their teachers and parents. Despite these powerful factors, many charter schools still struggle to fulfill the reform agendas that were dreamed of by their founders. Every philosophy is not equal. When granted the autonomy and authority required of true reform, the vision upon which Community of Peace Academy was founded holds great promise for transforming teaching and learning in public schools.

My partner, Mike Ricci, and I began working on the proposal

for Community of Peace Academy in May of 1994. There was no start-up money available, and so, with my husband's blessing, I took a year without pay in order to write and promote the proposal. Our home became my office, and our dining room table was piled high with every resource I could find. After nearly thirty years as a professional educator, when given the opportunity to found a school, one wants to get it right!

Having read widely and consulted a long list of educators whom I admired, the proposal was at last finished and approved. Experience had taught me that breathing life into the proposal depended upon the buy-in of the teachers and staff members who would be called upon to implement it. This, in addition to the fact that the teachers at Community of Peace Academy would have the controlling vote on the board of directors, made it imperative that teachers be intimately involved in all decisions regarding teaching and learning.

Since we had not yet located a facility, our first teacher interviews and early planning meetings were held at my home. Our staff included an ESL teacher, a young Hmong woman who would be our home–school liaison, two kindergarten teachers, two first-grade teachers, and one teacher for each of grades 2, 3, 4, and 5. My living room comfortably accommodated us, with some seated on pillows or on the carpet. Here, we met with representatives from textbook companies and peace programs and pored over curriculum materials throughout the summer of 1995.

Two of the teachers were Hmong women for whom this would be their first teaching assignment. Another was a recent graduate from Gustavus Adolphus College, my alma mater. Two were older women who were just beginning their teaching careers. All were teachers with great passion for the vision and mission of the school, but most had little classroom experience.

My professor at the University of St. Thomas reminded me that if the school was to become a true community of peace, the process of its development would need to be a peaceful one.

We knew that when school opened in September, 78 percent of our students would be Hmong. We were also aware that the Hmong had no written language until approximately sixty years ago. This and the fact that Hmong is a tonal language, similar to Chinese, would make the task of guiding our students to academic literacy in English a formidable challenge. Our budget to furnish an academic program for 160 students was $43,000. With this daunting task before us, I often reminded the staff that we were involved in a process, *a peaceful process*, and that we could not expect that everything would be perfect on the first day of school.

Teachers who joined the school that first year immediately recognized the implications of this unusual level of autonomy and ownership and its impact upon their work. Michele Conners, the most experienced teacher on the staff, with four years in diverse public schools in Houston, Texas, and three years teaching science for the St. Paul Public Schools, spoke of coming to an awareness shortly after beginning her career at Community of Peace Academy that "I'm really going to have to teach. . . . this is about more than crowd control." She attributed her 2001 Milken Award for Excellence in Teaching to her experience as a teacher at Community of Peace Academy: "I've had the freedom to develop my teaching skills that brought me to the point where somebody would consider me for that award."

In our first year, due to Mike Ricci's wisdom regarding the intense scrutiny that all new charter schools would, of necessity, need to endure, Community of Peace Academy applied for and received a grant from the General Mills Foundation to fund an outside evaluation of the school. Requests for proposals led us to Dr. Cheryl Lange of the University of Minnesota, who was hired as our professional evaluation consultant. That first year, Dr. Lange worked with a group of stakeholders to develop what would become our ongoing evaluation plan. Due to our focus on wholeness of life, the plan not only includes academic outcomes but also measures such things as school climate, attendance, parent satisfaction, and students' physical and emotional well-being and decision-making skills.

All decisions regarding teaching and learning are driven by the data provided in the annual evaluation report. Each year, Dr. Lange meets with the staff and board of directors to share the results of the evaluation process. Having heard the results, the staff immediately takes action. In this way, Community of Peace Academy remains in a constant and proactive school-improvement mode.

In the early years, a task force would meet throughout the summer to plan for the coming school year, based upon the evaluation results. In August, they would share their recommendations with the staff, and, having received input from all, changes would be implemented.

Each year, as the school has added the next grade or additional sections, the staff has grown. During the 2005–2006 school year, the staff totaled nearly one hundred. Along the way, it has become necessary to appoint committees to do much of the work that the original eleven staff members did together. Adjusting to this reality has not been without its challenges. By maintaining a high level of trust among all members of the staff, assuring adequate representation on each task force and committee, and keeping everyone well informed regarding committee recommendations, a process of decision making is being maintained that can bring about rapid change when needed and ensure staff support. Trust is the crucial factor, and maintaining this critical component requires unwavering commitment to the principles upon which the school was founded.

In 2001, the school hired a part-time literacy consultant, Dr. Nancy Healy, who later became the school's full-time instructional facilitator. Today the instructional facilitator works closely with the curriculum committee and staff development task force to guide our response to the data provided in our annual evaluation report.

Until 2003, Community of Peace Academy practiced looping. This strategy was included in the original proposal for the school to ensure that caring, trusting relationships would develop over time. Each teacher would have the same group of children for a two-year cycle: grades 1 and 2, 3 and 4, 5 and 6, or 7 and 8. In 1999, the school was offered federal class size reduction money, and a third first grade was added, lowering first-grade class size to sixteen. As a result, it was no longer possible to loop grades 1 and 2. Later, teacher certification requirements made it impossible to continue our practice of looping at grades 7 and 8.

In 2003, due to rigorous academic requirements under the No Child Left Behind legislation and the increased pressure of state testing, some teachers who were still practicing looping began a discussion about the possibility of abandoning the practice. They believed they could better master the academic curriculum and implement new initiatives more effectively if they focused on only one grade rather than two. Because we knew that looping had great potential to foster trusting relationships between teachers and their students, teachers could not reach agreement on the decision to continue or abandon it. In 2004, after careful consideration of the many effective initiatives in place at Community of Peace Academy to ensure that trusting, caring relationships prevail, I made a rare administrative decision to abandon the practice of looping. Such decisions cannot be taken lightly. Reformers must always be on guard against outside pressures, to make certain that we remain true to our most fervently held beliefs.

What did not change was the strength of the teams that teachers had formed in support of looping. Since 1996, Title I funds have provided guest teachers to free classroom teachers for a full day of team planning each month. Today all academic teams—kindergarten, grades 1 and 2, grades 3 and 4, grades 5 and 6, grades 7 to 12 English and social studies, grades 7 to 12 math and science, specialists (computer, physical education, music, and art), as well as the ESL and special education teams—have monthly planning days.

The instructional facilitator, ESL and special education teachers regularly hold meetings with classroom teachers on planning days.

In addition to these monthly planning days, the grades 7/8 team and the high school team meet weekly throughout the school year. Meetings of the K–8 staff are held less frequently. Teachers continually share their combined wisdom and creativity for the benefit of the learning community and students. In this way, best practices are routinely implemented and updated. Minutes from team planning days are submitted each month. The following planning day minutes, submitted by the third- and fourth-grade team, are typical:

GRADES THREE/FOUR PLANNING DAY: WED., OCT. 12, 2005

Present: Maren Goerss, Marcie Harris, Kirstin Molden, Paula Sanchez, Yoon Kee Tan

AGENDA:

TIES-TSIS

Bonnie and Katy helped the team log into the new TSIS student information system. The team hopes to be able to access student basic information.

St. Kate's Student

Ms. Goerss would like to host the student from St. Catherine's. She will discuss it with Dr. Rusthoven.

2005–2006 Team Goal

We have been working on writing for the past two years. We would like our new goal to center on Math. We will implement Calendar Math and Math Facts effectively and efficiently.

- We will plan ways to get all students involved (individuals and groups).

- We will determine benchmark levels.

- We will set aside time each week for practice and testing.

- Students will monitor their progress.

- We will pull vocabulary words from Minnesota Comprehensive Assessment sample tests to familiarize the students with this vocabulary.

Meeting with Instructional Facilitator

We reviewed our team goals and ideas. We will address progress toward our goals each planning day.

Conference Notes

Discussed the importance of diagnosing and teaching to student's needs. The more specific we can get to a child's needs the better the success.

Barbara Taylor

Teachers that used higher level questioning and got higher level responses from kids saw a lot of progress on standardized tests.

Developed Math Facts Practice and Testing Log

Maren shared a plan for a Math Facts Log that could be used during Morning Work.

New Report Card Sample

Discussion about Reading section of the report card. We decided that three sections would work best. Kirstin shared our ideas with Dr. Healy.

Arlington Library Books

We went to the Arlington Library and went through books that were being withdrawn from their library. We have added several books to our classroom libraries!!!

Respectfully,
Paula Sanchez

➤

The following initiatives are part Community of Peace Academy's ongoing school improvement efforts.

SHELTERED INSTRUCTION OBSERVATION PROTOCOL (SIOP)

In September of 2002, grade level teams (K, 1/2, 3/4, 5/6, 7/8, 9/12) began a series of Book Study sessions using the book *Making Content Comprehensible for English Language Learners: The SIOP Model*. These sessions were facilitated by the ESL teachers assigned to each team. This book and model of staff development was chosen to assure that all classroom teachers would be skilled in teaching English language learners.

In September 2003, Community of Peace Academy contracted with the ESL Department at Hamline University for ongoing staff development in use of the SIOP model. A professor from Hamline mentored classroom teachers in use of the SIOP model throughout the 2003–2004 school year.

Since then, teachers have continued to use the SIOP model. Lesson plans include content and language objectives and are shared with ESL teachers on Monday for their recommendations. The ESL teacher assigned to each team offers ongoing support. Teachers new to the school participate in a SIOP book study group facilitated by ESL teachers.

BALANCED LITERACY PROGRAM

In 2002, Community of Peace Academy teachers implemented a balanced literacy framework, including at least ninety minutes of reading instruction each day, Month by Month Phonics in grades K–6, small-group literature circle reading instruction, and the Six Traits Writing model. Overall reading scores have steadily improved as a result.

READING RENAISSANCE: ACCELERATED READING PROGRAM

In August 2002, the Reading Renaissance: Accelerated Reader Program was introduced to Community of Peace Academy through a Technology Literacy grant. The grant included extensive staff development and ongoing coaching and support for teachers. All classroom teachers are fully trained in the fundamentals of ongoing diagnosis and intervention in support of Accelerated Reader.

Accelerated Reader is fully implemented at Community of Peace Academy in grades K–12. There are currently over 17,000 titles in the school library to support this guided independent reading program.

SIX TRAITS WRITING

In spring of 2003, fifteen members of the staff attended Six Traits Writing training. Six Traits, which encourages writing across the curriculum, was developed nearly twenty years ago by the Northwest Regional Education Laboratory.

Field-tested and researched for many years, it is now used internationally. Most teachers at Community of Peace Academy now use Six Traits Writing. The instructional facilitator offers ongoing coaching and support.

CONSTRUCTIVIST MATH: INVESTIGATIONS IN NUMBER, DATA, AND SPACE (K–5), CONNECTED MATH PROJECT (6–8), AND CORE PLUS (9–12)

During the 2001–2002 school year, the curriculum committee began investigating new math programs. Members of the committee were sent to the State Math Conference. Math specialists from the Department of Children, Families and Learning met with the committee and presented to the entire staff. Following this process, the decision was made to adopt a constructivist math program. The following curriculums were adopted: Investigations in Number, Data, and Space (K–5), Connected Math Project (6–8), and Core Plus (9–12). Additional support materials are provided as necessary (Everyday Counts, Today's Math, Math Facts in a Flash, Accelerated Math). These three curriculums are all research based and endorsed by the National Mathematics Council.

K–8 SCIENCE AND SOCIAL STUDIES

The FOSS kits are used to teach science, grades K–8. This hands-on program encourages experimentation and teaches the scientific method. Evaluation of academic performance has been classroom based.

Social studies have been predominantly textbook based (McGraw-Hill). The program was aligned with state standards in 2004–2005. History Alive!, an activity-based program, was added during the 2005–2006 school year.

THE ARTS

Music and visual arts are offered at all grade levels. Students in grades K–8 use Orff instruments and learn to play recorders. Students perform on Dedication Day in October, at a winter concert in December, the Spring Sing and Annual Meeting in May, and at graduation ceremonies.

The Academy Choir, directed by John Sorlien, is the pride of the school. Members of the choir practice daily. This group has performed at the Mall of America, on two occasions during National Charter School Week, and has given concerts in collaboration with The Plymouth Rockers, a senior citizens' choir from Plymouth, Minnesota, and with One Voice GLBT mixed chorus. During the 2006–2007 school year, the Academy Choir will participate in concerts with World Voices under the direction of Karle Erickson in December and with the Bowling Green University Concert Choir from Bowling Green, Ohio, under the direction of William Skoog in May.

SPORTS AND EXTRACURRICULAR ACTIVITIES

Community of Peace Academy offers fall and winter sports for grades 7–12: volleyball and basketball for girls and soccer and basketball for boys. Staff members have been generous in offering after-school clubs and activities. The following were offered during the 2005–2006 school year: Chess Club (grades 5–12), Running Club (7–12), Art Club (7–12), Student Councils (7–8 and 9–12), Hip Hop Club (9–12), Japanese Club (9–12), Mock Trial (9–12), Science Club (9–12), Guitar Club (9–12), Ukrainian Egg Decorating (5 to adults), Choraliers (6 to 8 chorus). In addition, Peer Mediation, supported by students from Hamline University Law School, Model United Nations, and History Day are offered each year at the high school. High school students publish a school newspaper several times each year and an annual K–12 yearbook. In this way, the academic and social lives of students are further enriched.

In support of the education of the whole person, Community of Peace Academy will dedicate a new gym/auditorium in the fall of 2007.

TECHNOLOGY

All of Community of Peace Academy is wired for both local area and wide area networks. In addition, a wireless system allows staff members to access the network from school-owned laptop computers. Both Macintosh and PC products are used so that students can work in both platforms. The e-mail system has become the primary means of communication among staff members. There is a written school policy and a security system for Internet use.

Classroom computers have been used for teacher preparation and communication, Accelerated Reader quizzes and diagnostic reporting, Math Facts in a Flash (also a Renaissance Learning program), as well as additional software that supports the curriculum. Two computer labs, one Macintosh for the K–8 and one PC for the high school, provide for instruction in technology uses as well as large group writing and research assignments.

During the 2004–2005 school year, two teachers were trained by TIES to further incorporate technology into the curriculum using digital movie cameras and DVDs. During the 2005–2006 school year, these teachers assisted in training other teachers in the use of these technologies.

Two programs are in process. They are Web-based curriculum mapping program and student information systems. The curriculum mapping (TechPaths) will align curriculum to standards and assessments across K–12. The student information system will be linked to the mapping to provide assessment data and grades for individual students or a class. It also has a powerful grade book and report card program that can be accessed from home by students, parents, and teachers. All data will be accessible with a password through a data warehouse. These systems together will make the use of data easier and more efficient. Teachers will be able to further see connections between curriculum and assessment, both formative and summative.

Each teacher also has a password and immediate access to the performance of their students on the Measures of Academic Progress from Northwest Educational Assessment. These tests are taken in the spring of each year or in the fall, if necessary for new students. Summer school students are also tested using the MAP.

Previous efforts have been successful in many ways. The majority of students have shown growth on the MAP tests. African American students have made adequate yearly progress in both reading and math. When the eighth-grade students took the 2005 Basic Standards test, 73 percent of them passed the reading portion—more than any previous year. The Sheltered Instruction Observation Protocol (SIOP) adopted for the ELL students has made a difference in how classroom instruction is delivered. The math programs have been aligned across K–12, and new hands-on, mathematical reasoning materials have been implemented over the past three years. These materials are aligned to the standards of the National Council of Teachers of Mathematics as well as the Minnesota State standards, though there are a few specific areas for which we will be seeking supplemental materials.

Each year, Community of Peace Academy students continue to make steady progress toward excellence in reading, math, and writing. Eighth-grade Basic Standards Test results for 2005 are an example of this. Students must have passed these tests in order to graduate from high school. When limited English proficiency (L.E.P.) and economic factors are taken into consideration, these scores show great promise.

HIGH SCHOOL INITIATIVES

From the beginning, students attending Community of Peace Academy High School have been required to take four years of standards-based English, math, science, and social studies in addition to other state requirements. As the school has continued to grow and the program has continued to evolve, adjustments have been

2005 Eighth-Grade Basic Standards Test Results				
GROUP	L.E.P.	LOW INCOME	MATH	READING
Statewide	6%	29%	74%	85%
All of St. Paul	40%	73%	48%	65%
C. P. A.	56%	77%	63%	73%

made to meet the diverse needs of our students. Due to the influence of the peace and ethics focus of the school, it has proved to be a welcoming and effective academic environment for students with special needs. The excellent work of our special education team and a professional relationship with District 916, a provider of special education support and transition services, are helping to ensure the success of students with Individual Education Plans.

It is our goal that all students will graduate from high school, that all will pursue some form of postsecondary education, and that many will attend four-year colleges. For those who struggle academically, tutorials and an after-school homework club are offered. For those who are behind in credits, online courses are offered during the school year and during summer school.

A two-day planning retreat was held for the high school team in August of 2005 during which the theme for the year was chosen: "I am my future. I can succeed. I will do whatever it takes!" *Rethinking High School: Best Practice in Teaching, Learning and Leadership*, by Daniels, Bizar, and Zemelman (2001), was the focus of high school study groups throughout the 2005–2006 school year. *Subjects Matter: Every Teacher's Guide to Content-Area Reading*, by Daniels and Zemelman (2004), was read by a study group in 2004–2005. Harvey Daniels visited the school on May 17, 2006, and made a presentation to the high school team to further reinforce these best practices.

In August 2006, the high school team again held a two-day planning retreat. The topic under consideration was effective interpersonal communication. In addition, data was presented regarding the Hope Study survey, which was given to all high school students in fall of 2005 and spring of 2006. Developed by EdVisions, the Hope survey provides a means by which schools can be assessed as cultures that create a set of relationships, norms of behaviors, values, and commitments that lead to the development of healthy and productive students. Theory states that students in these sorts of supportive environments should respond by engaging more directly in their learning and, over time, gaining confidence in themselves as achievers (Eccles et al., 1993).

The Hope Study measures the degree to which the school context supports students' developmental needs for autonomy, belongingness, and a positive goal orientation. In addition, it measures student behavioral and emotional engagement in learning and their psychological adjustment, or "hope." Hope is a construct that reflects a student's perception of him- or herself as a success, a problem solver, and an achiever (Snyder et al., 1991).

Community of Peace Academy Hope Study results were highly encouraging. In the areas of belongingness and hope, scores were in the highest possible range. Autonomy scores were Good. Goal orientation scores were in the Good and Very Good range. Behavioral engagement was Fair, and emotional engagement was Very Good. This information affirmed the school's commitment to the education of the whole person.

STAFF QUALIFICATIONS

The executive director/principal holds an Ed.D. in educational leadership and a K–8 principal's license. The K–8 assistant principal holds an Ed.S. degree and a K–8 principal's license. The high school assistant principal holds an M.A. and a high school principal's license. The instructional facilitator holds a Ph.D. in reading instruction. During the 2006–2007 school year, Rob White, who has been a teacher at Community of Peace Academy since 1998, joined the leadership team to assist in facilitating the service-learning program and offer administrative support at the secondary level. Rob holds a master's degree and is in the process of completing a secondary principal's license.

Community of Peace Academy employs a diverse faculty of forty-six certified teachers. Of twenty-eight classroom teachers, all meet the No Child Left Behind standards for highly qualified teachers. Paraprofessionals met NCLB standards as well. Of fifteen general education paraprofessionals, all have two years of college and many have four-year degrees. All five special education paraprofessionals have four-year degrees. In addition, all K–12 teachers are trained in use of the Responsive Classroom program. There is a peaceful and focused academic environment at Community of Peace Academy. Student engagement is high. All teachers hold themselves to the professional standards set forth in the Framework for Teaching.

FRAMEWORK FOR TEACHING

During the 2001–2002 school year, Charlotte Danielson's Framework for Teaching teacher evaluation process was introduced to Community of Peace Academy. Throughout the school year and into the summer of 2002, a task force met to evaluate and revise the program. In August of 2002, a regional training for evaluators was held at Community of Peace Academy. A task force meets each year to continue to evaluate and update this program and to ensure ongoing staff support.

The Framework for Teaching, presented in the Association for Supervision and Curriculum Development book entitled *Teacher Evaluation: To Enhance Professional Practice*, is based upon a research-based set of teaching standards. After extensive study and deliberation, Community of Peace Academy has adopted the original

Framework rubrics as its guide to teacher evaluation and as the standard for best teaching practice. The school uses the original three-track system: Track I, novice teachers; Track II, experienced teachers; Track III, teachers in need of extra guidance and support. Track I teachers are observed at least twice annually. Track III teachers are observed at least three times. Track II involves self-monitoring, peer observations, and formal observations every third year. During the 2005–2006 school year, rubrics were developed by our ESL and special education teachers to more specifically guide their work.

STAFF DEVELOPMENT

The National Staff Development Council standards document recommends that staff development be data-driven, research-based, and evaluated using multiple sources.

Additionally, NSDC standards include three contextual elements: adults organized into learning communities, skillful school leaders guiding continuous improvement, and resources supporting adult learning and collaboration. These are in place at Community of Peace Academy.

In 2002, Community of Peace Academy made the decision to hire a full-time instructional facilitator. The instructional facilitator guides the work of the curriculum committee and the staff development task force. She reviews assessment data, meets with each team monthly, assists teachers in choosing classroom and student academic goals and provides ongoing staff development and support as needed.

All first-year teachers and teachers new to the school are provided a mentor. Mentors and Mentees meet weekly. Check lists are used to guide the process and to assure that all pertinent material is covered. Journals are kept and weekly reflections are written.

Each year, the staff development task force, made up of representatives of each team, prepares a calendar of staff development activities. Members of the task force examine all relevant data from the school's evaluation report to determine priorities. This extensive annual report is prepared by an outside consultant. Staff members are also surveyed. In recent years, staff development activities have included book study groups on a wide variety of topics, sessions related to specific curricular areas and teaching strategies and coaching and mentoring offered throughout the year in support of school wide initiatives such as Responsive Classroom and the SIOP model.

All members of the staff participate in the professional development activities planned by the task force. Each teacher also receives $500 each year to apply toward additional professional development related to his or her work. Paraprofessionals receive $250 for this purpose. Teachers are expected to take at least one professional day a year to participate in professional development activities outside the school.

The instructional facilitator maintains a resource room that includes professional books, videotapes, catalogs of instructional materials, and children's literature for guided reading instruction. These resources enhance both teaching and learning.

In a recent Association for Supervision and Curriculum Development publication titled *Results Now*, Mike Schmoker (2006) outlines a plan for achieving unprecedented improvements in teaching and learning. He recommends implementation of professional learning communities within traditional public schools: "The right image to embrace is of a group of teachers who meet regularly to share, refine and assess the impact of lessons and strategies continuously to help increasing numbers of students learn at higher levels." His recommendations are excellent: many of them have been implemented at Community of Peace Academy with great success. I agree with Schmoker's conclusion that if his recommendations were widely implemented, they could redefine public education and enable us to reach unprecedented levels of quality, equity, and achievement.

What Schmoker and most public education reformers fail to acknowledge is the importance of human relationships in the education process. As was my own experience, traditional public schools in which many teachers labor have no unifying moral vision, mission, or philosophy to guide them. Without a moral vision, schools often become dysfunctional and unhealthy communities in which adults do not practice or model caring and ethical human interaction. Under these circumstances, factions form, communication gives way to gossip, and most new initiatives are undermined. Working within these unhealthy communities drains one's spiritual and emotional energy. Some become cynical, pessimistic, negative, and bitter. Some leave the profession in disillusionment. Those who stay are frequently unable to inspire their students and give them hope, because their own spiritual and emotional resources are depleted. Within such an environment, sustained educational reform becomes impossible.

Without considerable attention to human relationships within our public schools, establishing and sustaining effective professional learning communities is unlikely. The autonomy offered by chartered public schools and the decision-making authority that they offer teachers would also greatly enhance the potential of Schmoker's recommendations becoming a reality.

Adherence to the new vision we are exploring has great potential to transform the work of teachers and thus lead to sustained positive education reform. Teachers frequently comment on ways in which their work at Community of Peace Academy has transformed their teaching. For example, Eric Fleming's personal philosophy of education changed as a result of his work at the school: "Honestly, when I came into Community of Peace Academy, I was excited about it, it seemed like a good fit, but my long term ambition I would say, was to get back into a private school setting. And having been here and having worked with the kids and the faculty and the specific ethics and moral education that we've been working on, and trying to improve and seeing the results of all these things, I've really become enamored with the program of the school, and my professional career, I think, has changed. I'm maybe a little more idealistic, in that I feel that a top level, or top quality education, can be had by anybody regardless of their background, and at Community of Peace Academy, the kids who come in here have that opportunity."

People whose work takes them to many public schools often comment on the positive effect that the founding principles have upon the learning environment at Community of Peace Academy. Sandy Naughton, a Ramsey County public health nurse, has provided family life classes at Community of Peace Academy since 1998. She commented: "The thing that is so striking about Community of Peace is the consistency of the staff and their constant modeling of respectful behavior with great expectations for the young people. Maybe that's the thing that stands out the most. There's an amazing amount of expectation coming from the teachers that the children here, can and will do well in every way; academically, ethically, the way they treat one another, the way they handle themselves."

Having once experienced the power of participation in such a moral learning community, teachers who move on to other professional endeavors, continue to appreciate the impact it had upon their personal and professional lives. On May 27, 2005, Jon Olson, former math teacher at Community of Peace Academy High School, sent the following e-mail to the high school team from his new post at Colegio Granadino in Colombia.

Dear High School Staff,

Each year as vacation draws near, I try to set aside some time to reflect on from where I have come and to where I am going in my teaching career. When I decided to become a teacher, I resolved to make my teaching experience meaningful and lasting. I still hold this resolve and reflecting helps me stay committed to it. Tonight,

I am remembering this time a year ago. I imagine you are all franti-cally finishing several projects with students or meticulously plan-ning graduation. I remember last year's graduation and my three years at CPA fondly.

My first year of teaching at Colegio Granadino will soon be history and my experiences at CPA and at Colegio Granadino have been markedly different. Articulating these differences is difficult, but I would like to share with you what I most admire about CPA. You are all aware that working at CPA is more than a job, more than simply teaching, or counseling, or performing administrative tasks. Yes, working at CPA is an experience far more complex and intense than any run-of-the-mill job. CPA is a place where, because of the great amount of time and of yourself that you dedicate to this work, disagreements are vehement and feelings are hurt. CPA also is a place where staff invite you into their house across the street when you lock yourself out of your car on a cold winter day, where your colleagues support you, and where your former students keep in touch despite the great distances that separate you. CPA is about relationships.

In April of 2000 I flew from Seattle to Minneapolis to interview for a math teaching position with a charter school, sans licensed math teacher, called Community of Peace Academy. At the time there were two high school teachers, Sean Acker and Eric Fleming. The former, after a lengthy panel interview, gave me a tour of the school. As we visited classrooms and walked the halls, Sean spoke clearly about the vision of the high school and the mission of CPA. While most school administrators or teachers who interview me speak of curriculum standards, scope and sequence, student-directed learning, or some other 50 cent word that educators coin, Sean spoke of relationships.

Detailing what I admire about each of you would take too much time, so I will briefly highlight your accomplishments as a team.

Firstly, CPA staff make decisions together. This I believe is your most significant accomplishment and one that I believe is critical to the long-term viability of the school. I felt more empowered to effect change at CPA than anywhere else I have worked. Secondly, you are a group of damn smart people! The average CPA staff IQ has to be at least two, maybe even two and a half, standard deviations above the mean. (No offense intended, Cara. I know IQ is not the most important measure of a person's potential and that standardized tests, while perhaps providing useful measurable information about a person, only further separate and denigrate us as human beings. But, damn, you all are smart!) And considering the intense scrutiny as you are under, I am surprised that this has not been published in the papers, yet. Thirdly, you are humble because none of you would ever publicly state how smart you are. Finally, you are brought together by a common vision. Staff at many schools struggle with unity because they lack a common vision, but your relationships are cemented by what you dream that your school, your country, and your world will someday be.

This is what is most special and endearing about CPA—that unexpectedly, someday while you are doing your job, you have an interaction with someone that makes you feel like everything is right with the world and that someway, somehow you played a part in bringing about this rightness. I remember feeling this way a few times while I was at CPA. Perhaps some of you are leaving CPA this year or perhaps you plan to work at CPA for several years to come. I encourage you to continue your work, wherever you may be, because it is good work and you do it exceptionally well!

Suerte y ánimo,
Jon Olson

What most often sabotages the efforts of public school reformers is lack of attention to human relationships within the school. The new vision I am proposing for America's public schools creates the

conditions for positive, sustained transformation of public education. Being given the autonomy to follow such a vision, and fully
embracing and implementing it, unleashes amazing potential.
Fueled by unconditional positive regard for all and a true sense of
ownership, an endless stream of wisdom, creativity, commitment,
and dedication is unleashed. The results are authentic, student-
focused, sustained academic improvement. Within such moral
learning communities, there is potential for every person to find
wholeness and fullness of life.

PART IV

Building I–Thou Relationships

Truth is found as we are obedient to a pluralistic reality, as we engage in that patient process of dialogue, consensus seeking, and personal transformation in which all parties subject themselves to the bonds of communal troth. Such a way of knowing is more likely to bridge our gaps and divisions than drive us farther apart. Such a way of knowing can help heal us and our broken world.

PARKER J. PALMER,
TO KNOW AS WE ARE KNOWN:
EDUCATION AS A SPIRITUAL JOURNEY

CHAPTER 14

Overcoming Fear

Mr. Xiong speaks for the first time. "Let me tell a story. This is not about people, it is about animals, but I think it is the same. When I was in Laos, I was attacked by six dogs. Even to this day, I am afraid of dogs. Even if I see a little tiny dog, I feel fear. I force myself now to reach out to dogs and to pet them. My neighbor has a dog and I talk to it and pet it and it likes me very much. We have to work to overcome our fears with people, too."

⟶

November 30, 1999

I am taking advantage of a break in the early-morning activity to check my voice mail messages when Lou Trudeau, the assistant principal, steps into my office. Lou informs me that there has been a confrontation between one of the teachers and a ninth-grade student. It happened at the end of the day yesterday as the buses were leaving. The student is Long Kue and the teacher is Aaron Benner. It is Aaron's first year at Community of Peace Academy, and he is the only African American teacher on our staff. Long is the oldest of the four Kue brothers. They are Hmong, and they have been students at our school since it opened in 1995. Lou goes on to say that the confrontation had ugly racial overtones. We agree that a meeting must be arranged immediately. Mr. Benner has a free period at 11:30 A.M., and so it is arranged. Although Lou usually handles disciplinary issues, I want to be present because of the extremely serious nature of the incident. We agree to meet in my office.

At 11:30 Long arrives. I ask him to be seated, and he slumps into a chair. His attitude seems quietly defiant. Lou calls to say that he is tied up in one of the classrooms and we agree that I will handle the meeting. I have asked Wang Xang Xiong, who is our home–school liaison, to attend the meeting. He is a gentle, compassionate man and father of eight. I want Long to feel supported. I call Mr. Xiong to tell him that Long has arrived. Rik Svien, one of the ninth-grade teachers, arrives next and finally Aaron. We greet one another and when all are settled, I begin the meeting.

I look directly at Long. He is a lean, attractive young man. His appearance reminds me that he is no longer a child. "Long, I understand that there was a problem yesterday between you and Mr. Benner after school on the bus. I understand that this seemed to be a racial problem. Because this is so against what we are trying to teach at our school, and because you have been a student here since the very beginning, and because you are now in the ninth grade and are becoming a young man, this is very serious to me. That's why I wanted to get together to talk about it right away. I've asked Mr. Xiong to join us so that if you want to express yourself in Hmong you can. Mr. Xiong can interpret for us." Long is listening intently and rubbing his hands nervously. He nods. He says something to Mr. Xiong in Hmong, and Mr. Xiong nods.

I admit that I do not know any of the details of the incident, and I ask who would like to begin. Aaron Benner responds. Mr. Benner teaches fifth grade. Remarkably, he was my student when he was in the fifth grade, and I was a teacher at St. Luke's Catholic School. He is a young man of impeccable character.

Mr. Benner explains that the incident began yesterday afternoon when he had to correct a group of ninth-grade boys who were roughhousing in the boys' lavatory next to his classroom. He explains that while Long was in the lavatory at the time, he was not involved in the horseplay. However, Long became very defensive and disrespectful toward Mr. Benner. Aaron assists with supervision of buses and approached Long outside at dismissal to clarify what had happened. Once again, Long was defensive and very disrespectful. Aaron later got on the bus to talk to Long, and the situation intensified. When Mr. Benner left the bus, Long apparently made derogatory racial remarks that were overheard and reported by other students.

Mr. Benner then addresses Long directly: "You treated me as if I were a ninth-grade student. I am a teacher. When I approached you, you tapped your chest like this, as though you were getting ready to fight me. I could see how upset you were. I wasn't even mad at you! You weren't one of the kids who were horsing around. You just happened to be in the lavatory at the time. I came up to you after school because I wanted to discuss this with you, and you continued to treat me as if I was a kid. I may look young, but I am a teacher. You need to treat me as you would treat any other adult. My students told me this morning that when I got off the bus you called me racial names. They were very upset."

Now I address Long. "Long, I have known Mr. Benner for a long time, and he is a very good person. I have known you for a long time, too, and I know that you are also a very good person. Mr. Benner is a teacher. He has worked hard to get to where he is, and he deserves your respect. All of us sitting here have worked hard to get to where we are. It is not easy, and all of us deserve your respect. Do you want to say anything?"

Long has been listening intently. He pauses and struggles to gain his composure. "Yes, I do." He is fighting tears and his words come slowly and deliberately. He addresses Aaron: "In the neighborhood where I live there are lots of Black kids. They are mean to me and they call us names and want to fight us all the time." Aaron responds: "I figured that that was the case. I am really glad you told me this. I am not one of those kids. You don't even know me. I'm an adult. I wasn't even mad at you. I just wanted to talk to you."

I turn to Long again. "I don't know what your experiences with

Black people have been, but I do know this. You are becoming a man. One of the things that I hope for you and for all of our students is that you will learn to accept each person as an individual. When we look only at outward appearances, we often miss opportunities to know some wonderful people. I want your life to be full of those opportunities."

Mr. Xiong speaks for the first time. "Let me tell a story. This is not about people, it is about animals, but I think it is the same. When I was in Laos, I was attacked by six dogs. Even to this day, I am afraid of dogs. Even if I see a little tiny dog, I feel fear. I force myself now to reach out to dogs and to pet them. My neighbor has a dog and I talk to it and pet it and it likes me very much. We have to work to overcome our fears with people, too."

Long addresses Aaron again. "I'm sorry I disrespected you. I know it was wrong." Aaron responds, "I accept your apology." Mr. Svien asks, "Could I make a suggestion? Because so many students witnessed your disrespect, Long, it would be good if they could see that you have made peace with Mr. Benner. It might be helpful if you could visit with each other at dismissal today." Long nods. Mr. Benner and Mr. Svien need to return to their classrooms, and they excuse themselves.

When they are gone, Mr. Xiong says, "I would like to speak to Long in Hmong." I indicate my approval and he begins. He talks to Long earnestly in a gentle, fatherly voice for what seems like a long time. Long's own father is absent from the home, and Long is listening intently and still dabbing at tears. When Mr. Xiong finishes, he looks at me and explains. " I was talking to Long about the importance of forgiveness." Now I address Long. "Long, I like you very much. I have always respected you, but I want you to know that after today, I respect you more than ever. I know that this was not easy for you. You were very honest, and I appreciate what you said. Think about what Mr. Xiong and Mr. Svien said. I hope that you and Mr. Benner will get to know each other because

I think you would 'really like each other. You can go back to class now. Have a good day."

Two weeks later a student appears at my office door carrying a bag and a note from Mr. Benner. It reads:

Ms. Rusthoven,

Could you please do me a big favor? I was hoping that you could call Long Kue to your office and tell him to choose one of these athletic hats in the bag. You can tell him it's a gift from me if you want. He has been so polite and always stops to ask how I'm doing when he sees me in the halls. I truly believe he is sincere.

Thank you,
Aaron

Racial and cultural intolerance and conflict are most often based upon ignorance and fear. Simply punishing students who act on their ignorance and fear will not change what is in their hearts. Racial incidents, such as the one described in this narrative, are common in schools serving diverse students and staff. This defines most public schools in America. We adults must assist our students in growing beyond their prejudices and overcoming their fears. Our response to conflict has the potential either to add fuel to the fire or to profoundly change the school culture and our students' hearts and lives for the better.

CHAPTER 15

Searching for Truth

Yonas looks completely serious as he listens. He becomes tense and shifts in his seat as if this news weighs very heavily upon him. When I am finished, he says, "I know what this is about. I know exactly what this is about." His voice is quiet and he is defensive. He is searching for the right words with which to begin. He says, "I am not surprised by this. This is nothing new. This has been going on ever since I came." After a long hesitation, he says, "Well, I might as well tell you this. I probably should have come to you long ago."

—◆—

September 13, 2000

It is a lovely, sunny, late-summer day. It is nearly time for dismissal, and I am in my office with Wang Xang Xiong, our home–school liaison, and Yao Yang, Ka Lee's mother. Yao has asked to see me, and since I do not speak Hmong and Yao does not speak English, Wang Xang will be our interpreter. After we exchange greetings, Yao begins and Wang Xang interprets for me. He tells me that Ka has asked Yao to talk to me about the Black man who is teaching math to the tenth grade. She is concerned because he is not challenging Ka enough. He also does not explain the work clearly. He writes the work on the board, and he expects the students to figure it out without any explanation. This is difficult not only for Ka but for many students. Therefore, Yao is not only representing Ka in coming to me. The other students know that she often comes to school, and so they have asked her to speak for them as well. I take this to mean that there is the force of many behind Yao's concern regarding the math teacher, and I try to assure her that I will take her concern seriously. I thank her for telling me and say that I will talk to the teacher right away.

As soon as Yao and Wang Xang have gone, I decide to go outside to find the math teacher, Yonas Ghebregzi. Yonas is Eritrean, and I was first introduced to him by my husband, Jay, in late February of 2000. The day that Jay met Yonas, he came home and enthusiastically informed me that he had met someone that I really needed to meet. He informed me that Yonas was a well-educated man with a degree in engineering from the University of Minnesota and that he had taught high school math and science in Eritrea. Furthermore, my husband thought he might be interested in working at Community of Peace Academy.

I had recently learned that Rik Svien, our high school math and science teacher, would not be returning for the next school year and that he was feeling somewhat overwhelmed in trying to meet the varied needs of our students. We had decided to hire a teacher's assistant to assist Rik until the end of the year, and so I called Yonas the next day.

My interview with Yonas confirmed what my husband had told me. He was a bright and articulate man who seemed to embrace the philosophy and mission of the school, and he was interested in joining the staff. We hired him as a teacher's assistant to the math and science teacher, and according to the teacher, Yonas's work was excellent. He was hired to assist in teaching summer school, and after two failed attempts to find a certified math teacher for the 2000–2001 school year, we were able to acquire State Board of Teaching approval to hire Yonas as a community expert to teach high school math and science. Yao's complaint came on the seventh day of the school year.

I am happy for an excuse to get outside. Dismissal is almost a festive time on these sunny afternoons. Teachers and students greet one another, talk and laugh as students either wait in line or rush to board their buses. Dismissal takes longer the first few weeks of school as someone's bus is nearly always late. This fact has worked to my advantage today. I find Yonas with his daughter, who is a new kindergartner. He, too, is smiling. I ask if he has time to stop by my office, and since he is free, we go directly there. His daughter comes with us.

We each take a seat at my small octagonal table and I begin. I explain that Ka's mother has come to see me and that she is concerned about the math. Ka has asked her mother to come because she does not think she is being challenged enough. I tell Yonas that her message was somewhat contradictory, because she also said that Ka did not understand the math and that the teacher did not explain it, but expected students to figure it out for themselves. I also tell him that Yao said that she was bringing this concern not only for Ka but also on behalf of many other students.

Yonas looks completely serious as he listens. He becomes tense and shifts in his seat as if this news weighs very heavily upon him. When I am finished, he says, "I know what this is about. I know exactly what this is about." His voice is quiet and he is defensive. He is searching for the right words with which to begin. He says, "I am not surprised by this. This is nothing new. This has been going on ever since I came." After a long hesitation, he says, "Well, I might as well tell you this. I probably should have come to you long ago."

Having made this decision, Yonas begins. He tells me that since the very first day, he has sensed the animosity of the Hmong students toward him. He talks about the animosity that he perceives most Hmong people feel for Africans and African Americans.

Yonas lives in a housing complex surrounded by many Hmong families. He tells me that his daughter told him that a certain Hmong word meant, "Come in," because whenever she would go to the home of a Hmong child they would say that word. He did some investigating and learned that the word in fact means, "Go away." He tells me that at our parent registration night the Hmong parents would not offer their hands to him. The Hmong students will not say good morning when he greets them in the hallways.

As president of the Student Council, Ka is a leader at the school. Yonas says that Ka has joined forces with Cindy, her best friend, and others. The girls will talk in Hmong around him and will laugh and make it very difficult for him during class. He tells me that his response to this has been to concentrate even more on teaching the subject. He tells me that a few of the boys have been more cooperative and that they are progressing well ahead of the others. Ka is now in the middle rather than at the top. Yonas feels that if Ka took the math more seriously, she too could be a top student. Cindy, on the other hand, needs much help and has flat out refused his assistance. He tells me that Cindy would rather sit and do nothing than have him help her, although he keeps offering.

As Yonas speaks, thoughts are flying through my mind with a dire urgency, but I am very thoughtful and choose my words carefully before I begin. I respect Yonas and I can feel his pain and frustration as he pours out this litany that has been building for so long. I look into his eyes. I know that Yonas is a person of faith, and so I decide to say what I really believe. "Yonas, God has sent you here for a reason. You have a more important job to do than the teaching of math." He lets out a chuckle that indicates surprise, confusion, and relief all at once. He nods and waits. I continue: "I am so glad that you are telling me this. This is very important information. We must deal with this head-on. If we allow this kind of behavior and look the other way, everything we are trying to teach at Community of Peace Academy is called into question. This simply is not OK."

As Yonas has discussed the rejection he has been experiencing, he likens it to the rejection he has experienced in many places and situations throughout his life. His demeanor is that of a proud man representing a proud people, and he takes a defensive, almost cold stance as he presents this information. As gently as I can, I draw attention to his body language. I let him know that as a teacher here at Community of Peace Academy, he must set his personal feelings aside. Our strongest commitment here is to lead our students to fullness of life for all. This cannot happen until prejudices of this type are overcome. He will need to teach by his example one of life's most challenging lessons: that it is not acceptable to disregard a person simply because he or she is not the same as you are. This will require that Yonas meet the students perhaps more than halfway. I offer to arrange a meeting between him, Ka and Cindy and to facilitate the discussion.

Yonas tells me that he is more than willing. He says that he is so pleased that we have had this discussion. He tells me that the situation has been troubling him for a very long time. He informs me that he was sure that none of the Hmong students would enroll at our school for tenth grade since he was going to be their teacher and that he was very surprised to see them on the first day. Then, after deliberating for some time, he decides to confide something that up until now, he has not told me. "I know that I should have told you this long ago, but I honestly didn't know if you could handle it. I know how you feel about the school, and I thought it would be very hard for you to hear this. I thought you would be very hurt by it."

Yonas tells me that until today, he did not realize how serious I was about this work. I tell him once again that the teaching of peace and ethics is the most difficult subject we teach at Community of Peace Academy and our most urgent challenge. If we don't get this right, the whole school is a sham.

The next morning I am about to leave for a doctor's appointment when Yonas comes to my office door and asks to speak to me. I invite him in. He is once again very serious. He tells me that he has been thinking constantly of our conversation and that he was not able to sleep last night. He is afraid for his daughter's safety, and he has to think about her first. He wants to talk with Ka and Cindy as soon as possible. We decide that we will meet with them at 1:20 that afternoon. He prefers that I meet with the girls first and then call him in, and so it is decided.

At 1:20 I call for Ka and Cindy. They are taking a test and the teacher says that he will send them as soon as they finish. When the girls arrive they look somewhat curious about the reason for the meeting. I know both of these girls well and think well of them. All of our interactions are positive and cordial. When we are seated, I inform them that Ka's mother came to see me yesterday to share their concerns about Mr. Ghebregzi—Mr. G., as he is known to them. I restate Yao's concerns and ask for their input.

Cindy is quiet and defers to Ka. Ka restates the concerns raised by her mother. She tells me that others also feel this way. Once again, I choose my words carefully. I begin by telling them how I came to know Mr. G. and why I hired him in the first place. I talk about his good character and his excellent knowledge of math. I then tell them that I have discussed their concerns with him, and I go on to share his concerns about them.

Ka looks somewhat sheepish and smiles at Cindy. Cindy looks more unyielding, as though she is not about to be swayed by my opinion of Mr. G. I talk to Ka about speaking Hmong in front of him, and she admits that she has done this and that her intentions were less than noble. Ka states that her behavior was not caused by racial prejudice, although she cannot quite articulate why she does not like Mr. G. I state that the wall they are putting up between them and their teacher is making it very difficult for him to teach them and that they have much to lose if they continue and much to gain if they can remove the wall. They agree to talk to Mr. G. and to work to make things better.

I then call Yonas and ask him to join our meeting. When he arrives it is clear that this is an uncomfortable moment for all. The girls are quiet ... waiting ... Finally, Yonas begins. He is visibly struggling to be open to them and to meet them in a conciliatory way. He talks about their ability and about his desire to teach them well. He says that it is his goal to prepare them so that they can have a better life. He tells them that the math program we are using is excellent and that if they master it, they will be prepared to attend any college. He talks directly to Cindy about the way she has chosen to shut him out. He congratulates her on passing her basic skills math test this summer but assures her that she could have had a much higher score had she been willing to accept the help that he offered. He talks to Ka about her present position in the class and informs her that if she chose to do so, she could be in a more challenging group. In the end, Ka requests that she be placed in that group and states that she is up for the challenge. Yonas agrees to honor her request. Cindy is noncommittal. At the conclusion, I ask if anyone has anything else they want to say. There is no response, and the meeting is concluded. Yonas thanks me and they leave to return to class. This will take time.

Two days later, when I see Yonas in the faculty room, he is smiling broadly. He reports that things are much better. "I am sleeping very well now," he tells me. As the days pass, it is apparent that a change in attitude has occurred. We have turned a corner.

Most people do not seek diversity. Life is easier when lived only with people who are just like us: the greater the difference, the greater the challenge. Living peacefully in a diverse community is hard work. Yet our world is a diverse place and growing smaller each year. Future citizens must embrace diversity.

Racial, ethnic and cultural diversity within our school community, expand our world-view and enrich our education. This is a founding principle of Community of Peace Academy. If we really believe this, we must make it a priority in our schools. We must open our hearts and our doors to diversity, and prepare both students and staff to venture into new territories beyond old comfort zones. Learning to accept difference, and to learn from it, leads to truth and wisdom.

CHAPTER 16

The Golden Rule

Again, William doesn't miss a beat. "He disrespects me and I disrespect him. Do to others as they do to you. That's what you teach us."

October 10, 2000

Once again, Yonas has come to see me regarding the attitude of a particular tenth-grade student. This time, it is William Walker. William is African American and has attended Community of Peace Academy since fifth grade. He has a learning disability and struggles with both academic and social issues.

The incident that Yonas brings to my attention occurred on Thursday, October 5, when Yonas was subbing for Sean Acker's tenth-grade astronomy class. During class, William was not listening. This is not unusual behavior for William, but to compound the problem, he was talking to Kalia and distracting her as well. Kalia usually listens. When Yonas asked William to stop talking and listen, William said, "Look around. No one is listening to you." He had also remarked in front of the class that Yonas was "just a teaching assistant and not a real teacher."

Yonas explained that he had talked to Kalia and that after that, she had been respectful and had participated. Later, he had tried to speak to William privately. William responded, "Why don't you take a survey. Nobody likes you around here." Yonas had talked to Stephanie, William's special education teacher and she advised him to "write him up." Yonas said that at the beginning of the year, during a morning meeting, William had remarked, "Our teachers are not the right teachers."

It was Yonas's opinion that William could be in a higher group if he could focus on his work. He reported that William is always talking and does not work during the study period that has been set aside each day. Further, Yonas heard that William had told another student that Yonas is a mean teacher. "I do not joke around with them," He tells me. "I help them with school work and ask them if they have school work to do. William feels like I'm breathing down his neck."

I tell Yonas that we need to meet with William as soon as possible to discuss his behavior and to let him know that it is not acceptable. We decide to meet at 11:35 that morning during X-period, the time set aside for study, individual meetings with students, and so on.

That same morning, I hear from Molly, our social worker. She tells me that she is very concerned for Yonas. She reports that he talked to her and that he seemed overwhelmed. He has told Molly that the kids won't accept him. He feels that it is due to his accent and culture. He believes that there are cultural barriers that the kids can't get past. Molly is wondering if she could talk to the tenth grade regarding cultural differences. Molly says, "I feel so sorry for Yonas. I'm surprised by this, but some of the kids have never experienced this kind of diversity. I don't know what they are being taught at home. I've never seen a staff person so dejected. I can't imagine what this must be like for Yonas."

At 11:35, Yonas and William arrive in my office. William nods and shakes my hand in greeting. Through the years we have established a very cordial relationship. When we are seated, I begin. "William, Mr. G. has told me that last Thursday when he was subbing for Mr. Acker, you were not listening. When he tried to talk to you about this later, you said, 'Take a survey. Nobody likes you around here.' What would you think if someone said that to you?"

Without hesitation and without malice, William responds, "I'd want to know why they didn't like me."

I am somewhat taken back by his response and I take a minute to think before I answer. "That may be true, but if someone said that to me, I'd feel hurt. It would seem like a putdown to me. Another thing that you must remember is that Mr. G. is a teacher. You owe him respect, and he owes you respect. If he had said the same thing to you, your parents could sue him."

Again, William doesn't miss a beat. "He disrespects me and I disrespect him. Do to others as they do to you. That's what you teach us."

This time I don't hesitate. I reach for the framed copy of the Golden Rule that is sitting on my desk at arm's length from where William is seated, and I turn it so that it is facing him. "No. It doesn't say, 'Do to others as they do to you.' It says, 'Do to others as you would have them do to you.' The Golden Rule is not about revenge."

I go on to tell William that Mr. G. has been hired to teach math and science because of his knowledge of both subjects and that he has much to offer. I tell him that Mr. G. has taught in his own country, Eritrea. I explain that in that country, everyone does not have the chance to go to school, so the students are very serious about school and respectful of teachers. Mr. G. is not used to having students waste their opportunity to get a good education. I ask, "How do you act in Mr. G.'s classes?" William answers honestly. "I don't listen." I ask, "Who will lose in the end if you keep this up?" "I will." Once again an honest answer. At this point, Yonas speaks. "William, I want you to know that I will not be celebrating if you do not succeed. I want you to succeed. You have the ability to be right at the top."

Once again William's answer catches me off guard. "I don't want to be at the top. I want to be right in the middle." He goes on to give a rationale for this decision. He doesn't want to be at the bottom, but he doesn't want to have to work too hard either. William speaks like a lawyer, with poise and confidence.

We tell him that he may regret such a decision in three years when he is out of high school and finds that he has limited his future choices. We encourage him to rethink this situation and to learn all that he can now so that he can do great things later on. We have the last word, but it doesn't feel like a victory.

In January, at our second annual College Fair, I run into William in the hallway with his arms full of college catalogs and materials. We have just listened to six recruiters advising our students to work hard and to do their very best if they hope to go to college. William tells me that he thinks he will go to Hamline and study law. I tell him that I think he would make an awesome lawyer. Then, I can't resist the temptation. "William, that reminds me of the conversation that we had with Mr. G. in my office that day." He doesn't miss a beat. "Will you just forget that conversation! That conversation never happened!" Humor is good for the soul.

EPILOGUE

On October 26, 2005, a panel of Community of Peace Academy alumni were invited to address the high school Ethics Forum regarding the 2005 High School Theme, "I Am my future! I Can succeed! I Will do whatever it takes!" William Walker was among them, having graduated with the class of 2003. The alumni were asked to respond to the following questions:

- ✦ Where are you now?

- ✦ What are you planning?

- ✦ How are you meeting your financial obligations?

- If you could go back to Community of Peace Academy, what would you do differently?

- What was helpful at Community of Peace Academy?

The graduates shared the struggles they face balancing work, school, and personal obligations. They spoke with pride about college life, holding jobs, having their own apartments and cars. Their words were candid and sincere, encouraging the underclassmen to work hard, to listen to wise people and to make every day count. Again and again they paid tribute to the staff for the attention and care they had received and spoke of the positive impact these relationships had had upon them. Not surprisingly, William was the most articulate and eloquent speaker.

Throughout the assembly, Yonas and the staff stood at the back of the gym listening intently. Near the conclusion of the forum, the discussion turned to the topic of the workload students could expect in college. William looked directly at Yonas. Banging his fist on the table with each exclamation, he stated, "You guys, I know Ghebregzi is intense! Intense! Intense! But, I want you to know, he's the best math teacher I ever had!" William's declaration was met with enthusiastic applause.

CHAPTER 17

Taking Time

Mr. Xiong interprets my words for Chue's mother and she speaks again. He tells me, "She wants to thank you for your patience and for your wisdom and your kindness in dealing with parents. In her other son's school, when the student is in trouble, the principal grabs them by their hair and drags them and there are police everywhere and she does not appreciate that."

January 9, 2001

On Monday, I am informed by Jeff Blevins, the computer teacher, that Sammy has "lost it" in the computer lab and has been sent to see me. Sammy tells me that he just can't handle this school. He tells me that he doesn't want to get out in the world and think that everybody loves everybody and that everybody is supposed to be nice all the time. He says that he is an eye for an eye and a tooth for a tooth sort of guy.

Sammy joined our tenth grade in October and it has been a culture shock for him. I decide to let him talk. He goes on to recall his behavior at his former school. He is not used to being a good kid—doing his work, following rules, being respectful. He tells me that now I'm probably going to say, "If you don't like our rules, then leave." He says that's what they always say. He tells me that every day when he goes home his mom has a big smile on her face. She asks him how he did in school today and he tells her,

"Just fine." He doesn't want to take that away from her. He says that he thinks it would be easier if he just got kicked out of here. He has done that before. I sit quietly and listen. He talks on and on. Finally he looks at me and says, "I don't know what you want me to do. What am I supposed to do now?"

Obviously, Sammy is feeling compromised. I tell him that his mother is a big girl and that if he really doesn't want to be here, he needs to tell her. I tell him that his anger in the computer lab was not really about what Mr. Blevins asked him to do. He agrees and says he will apologize to Mr. Blevins. He says he will talk to his mother. I give him a pass and he leaves. I inform Molly and ask her to follow up with Sammy on Friday.

Two days later, I receive notice that there has been a fight involving our two new tenth-grade students, Sammy and Chai. It is 1:20. Apparently the fight occurred in the hallway as the students were on their way to class after lunch. Sammy has been brought to my office, and Chai is waiting in the business office reception area. I ask Mr. Xiong to call Chai's parents to come for him and to arrange a meeting. I call Sammy's mother. It seems that the rare fights that occur here most often involve new students. In this case, I am sorry to hear that Chue Vang was also involved. This is a major violation. Chue has been a student here since the school opened in 1995. Chue should know better.

Mr. Xiong also calls Chue's mother, and she says that she will come immediately. While we are waiting, I give Chue a sheet of paper and ask him to write down what happened. He writes: "I got involved because I pushed Sammy and I took a jab at him once. That's how I got involved." Not much information there.

I talk briefly with Sammy. He tells me that the fight involved Jacque. Jacque came to our school last year, and she and Sammy are friends. Chai had made a derogatory remark about Jacque based upon something that happened outside of school, and Sammy had told her about Chai's remark. Chai threatened to fight, and Sammy finally put down his books. Chai took the first punch, but it quickly became apparent that Sammy was in control. That's when Chue stepped in to help Chai. Sammy reports that he was shocked when Chue hit him. He never thought Chue would do a thing like that, and he can't understand why he did it.

Chue's mother soon arrives. She is a fully supportive parent, and over the years I have come to respect her wisdom. She speaks no English and I do not speak Hmong, so we must rely on Mr. Xiong to interpret. I ask Chue to tell us what happened. He says that it happened so fast—he just joined in. I ask Chue if he understands what Sammy and Chai were fighting about. From his answer, it is apparent that Chue knew that tension had been building between Sammy and Chai.

I talk to Chue about the fact that peace building is difficult. It is a choice we make. I ask what other choices he might have made. He says that he could have broken up the fight . . . he could have gone for an adult. Of course, I knew what Chue would say before I asked. He knows what we teach. I talk about the fact that we teach these things to prepare our students to act in times of crisis, not when it is easy. We practice peace-building skills in grade school to prepare for adulthood. Mr. Xiong interprets my words for Chue's mother. She responds and he interprets her message for me. She agrees with everything I have said. She wants Chue to be friends, to make peace, not to fight.

I tell Chue that Sammy has told me that he did not want to fight Chai. I also tell him that Sammy was very surprised when Chue joined Chai in fighting Sammy. I ask Chue if he would be willing to talk to Sammy about what happened. He shrugs.

Mr. Xiong now speaks directly to Chue in Hmong for what seems like a long time. When he is finished, he interprets for me. He has told Chue that he has been here long enough—he needs to be a good role model. He needs to be the one who tries to stop the fight and seek a wise person. Chue should help make peace even if he gets hurt in the middle. Mr. Xiong has told Chue that since

Hmong are the majority at our school, they need to be careful of this. He has reminded him that in Laos, Hmong wanted independence and peace. Now they must work for peace in this country.

We move on to the Contract for Resolution of a Violation. Under Plan of Action/Measurable Goals, we write, "Chue and Sammy will meet with Mrs. Rusthoven to resolve what happened between them. If Chue suspects trouble of any kind in the future, he will leave the situation and find an adult." We decide to have a follow-up meeting in two weeks, Tuesday, January 23, at 8:30 A.M. Following the meeting I talk to Molly, our school social worker. I ask her if she would be willing to meet with Chai and Sammy. She agrees.

As days slip by, I am aware that I have not met with Chue and Sammy. I procrastinate, reasoning that since we have met with each of them and their parents individually, and since we have written behavior agreements for each of them, they will be fine. Besides, knowing Sammy and Chue, I am quite sure that they would not fight again. I check with Molly, and she has met with Chai and Sammy. I am pleased and grateful.

On the morning of January 23, at 8:30, Chue and his mother arrive for our follow-up meeting as scheduled. I begin by recounting why we are gathered, and I review the contract. I then admit to all present that I did not meet with Chue and Sammy as I said that I would. I apologize for this and ask Chue if he and Sammy have talked since the fight. Chue tells us that he and Sammy have not talked. I ask if he feels threatened by Sammy. He says that neither he nor Sammy feels threatened by the other and that they are not angry with one another, but that they just don't talk. Chue agrees that he will continue to follow the contract. He will report to an adult if he suspects trouble.

Mr. Xiong interprets this for Chue's mother. She begins to speak. Mr. Xiong interprets. "She requests that you meet with Chue and Sammy so that they will not be shy with each other and can be friends." Once again, I am impressed by the wisdom of Chue's mother. I thank her for asking that I do this and I assure her that I will meet with the boys today. Had she not requested it, I would not have taken the time.

Mr. Xiong interprets my words for Chue's mother, and she speaks again. He tells me, "She wants to thank you for your patience and for your wisdom and your kindness in dealing with parents. In her other son's school, when the student is in trouble, the principal grabs them by their hair and drags them and there are police everywhere and she does not appreciate that."

Immediately following the morning announcements, I call for Chue and Sammy. We sit at the table in my office. I sit in the middle facing the wall, and Chue and Sammy sit on opposite sides of the table facing each other. I tell Sammy that I had intended to get them together following the fight and had not done so. I let him know that at Chue's follow-up meeting today, his mother requested that we meet. I ask the boys if they know each other. Chue shakes his head, and Sammy says, "Not really." I tell them that I feel that I know both of them and that I like them both very much and think that they would like each other if they knew each other.

Sammy asks Chue why he hit him. "Why did you do that? I didn't think we had any problems with each other. I was just really surprised when you hit me."

Chue says that he did it to help Chai. "You were so much bigger than him. I just did it to help him."

Sammy says, "You've got to know something about me. I don't like to fight. If I see even the slightest expression of fear on the other guy's face, the fight is over. I can't stand to see anybody look afraid."

Chue is listening, smiling. "You just looked really mad and it all happened so fast, I just jumped in."

"I wouldn't have hurt him, man," Sammy says. "I could see how you might have thought that, though."

I suggest that each of the boys tell the other some good things about himself. They look sheepish and somewhat uncomfortable. After a minute, Sammy begins. "Well, before I smoked, I used to like sports." They both laugh. Sammy says, "I can tell you something good about you. You've got the cutest girlfriend in the whole school and everybody knows it!" They laugh again, and Chue seems pleased by the compliment. This activity has loosened them up and they begin to talk as if I weren't there.

They talk easily back and forth discussing the fight and all that led up to it. Sammy tells Chue that Jacque is a good friend of his and that he wanted her to know what Chai had said, because she needed to stay away from Chai. Chue said that he was just looking at how big Sammy was and because Chai is Hmong, he wanted to help him. Sammy said that his dad always taught him to defend himself, but he doesn't start fights and he doesn't like to fight.

I tell both boys that each of us chooses how we will be in the world. I tell them that I believe it is possible to go all through your life and never have a physical fight. To do this, we practice solving our problems with our head instead of our fists. I remind them that how we live our lives has to do with choices that we make, including who we choose as friends. I realize that I am preaching. Enough has been said. This has been an important meeting, and I'm glad that Chue's mother insisted upon it. Chue and Sammy have at least acknowledged one another. It is a beginning.

Guiding the moral development of our nation's youth *takes time*. Too many middle and high schools are huge, impersonal institutions where angry students parade in and out of the principal's office every five minutes, with no hope of positive change. Our public schools must be structured to accommodate this life-changing work. In truth, there are no shortcuts available to our nation. Either we will make the necessary investment of time and resources available now and restructure our public schools to effectively pursue this important work, or we will be forced to invest even greater amounts of time and resources later, with no redeeming results.

CHAPTER 18

Lions and Lambs

Once again I address Bla directly. "What do you think these boys see when they look at you?" She shrugs. "They see a very beautiful young girl. And they want you very badly. But they want you the way the lion wants a lamb. They want you not because they care about you. They do not care about you at all. They want you for what they can get from you. When they look at you they see money. You are valuable to them. Gangs sell young girls for sex. They can make one hundred, maybe two hundred dollars every time you have sex with someone. They use the money to buy expensive cars and drugs. It is their business and they are very good at it.

March 23, 2001

March came in like a lion. After several mild Minnesota winters, snow banks reached six feet, and six inches of ice accumulated on sidewalks. Spring arrived on Tuesday and the temperatures soared into the forties. Spring break is just one week away. Spring break can be a dangerous time.

This morning I held the third of what will be five parent meetings with Hmong parents and their eighth-grade daughters. The past two weeks have been unsettling. This particular situation began last Thursday in the cafeteria. A group of Hmong girls had a loud confrontation during which gang threats were exchanged. Tim McGowan investigated the incident and found that one of the girls had a "slam book" in which had been written many gang-related statements and threats. Upon further investigation, several slam books were found. These discoveries led to a number of meetings with the girls and in the end, one of them was sent home until a meeting could be arranged with her parents. Because there was much data to investigate, we decided to wait until Monday to determine what should be done about the involvement of the rest of the girls.

On Tuesday, there was another major altercation at the end of the day, this time in the girls' lavatory. It involved a loud shouting match, swearing, and gang-related threats. Three girls were suspended, and one more had been sent home on Tuesday for statements written in her slam book.

This is not the first time we have been confronted with gang-related activity at school, nor is it the most severe gang related activity we have encountered. We are well versed regarding gangs and what they do. In the past, however, these incidents have involved one student at a time. The fact that so many girls seem to be involved in this situation causes us great concern.

At present, we are working with a boy who has made a decision to "get out" and to have his gang tattoo removed. His future is becoming more hopeful, but it will continue to be a struggle for him. Just two years ago, we lost a student to a gang over spring break. The story of her dramatic comeback is all too rare. After a long struggle to recapture the heart of another student, we finally lost him to his gang last year. Our successes related to gang issues have been largely due to the assistance we have received from Kevin Navara, Ramsey County sheriff and member of the Hmong Gang Strike Force. We are up against a formidable enemy, and we know it.

As we review our Family Handbook, it becomes clear that we have not stated a policy specific to gang activity. Since there is nothing more dangerous that a student could do, we determine that any activity related to gangs must be treated as a major violation. The student will be sent home until a meeting can be arranged with his or her parents. Since so many girls are involved in this, we decide that the consequence will be a two-day suspension. Meetings will be conducted with each of the girls and their parents before they return to school on Monday.

Because this interest in gangs seems to be so pervasive, we decide to call a meeting of all of the girls and their parents as well. This will be held in the library next week on Tuesday evening at 6:00. We mail a letter regarding the meeting to each family, in English and in Hmong. I send an e-mail to Kashia Moua asking her to help us with the meeting. Kashia conducts weekly meetings of Hmong Woman's Circle with our eighth-grade girls. She created this very effective program for Hmong girls in response to the tragic murder of her cousin. Kashia returns my message. She will be out of town next Tuesday, but she tells me that she can meet with me on Thursday to help plan the meeting. I am grateful. We decide to get input from Kevin Navara as well. The meeting with Kashia is productive.

My busy week is punctuated with four intense and emotional parent meetings for the purpose of reinstating the girls who have been suspended: one on Wednesday, one on Thursday, and two on Friday. Two of the meetings require that Mr. Xiong interpret; two do not. Each time, I begin by stating that it has come to our attention that a number of girls in the eighth grade have been involved in writing gang-related statements and in making gang-related threats. I state our "no tolerance" policy, which is due to the danger and seriousness of gang activity. I then speak directly to the student and ask her to tell us why she thinks we are having this meeting.

Bla Chang's meeting is typical. She tells us that Sheng Her called her friends and told them that if they call Bla anymore, Sheng will get her gang to beat them. Bla says that she became angry about this and was yelling and swearing at Sheng in the bathroom. The conversation goes something like this:

"Who are these friends that Sheng called?"

"Ying, Richard, and Pao."

"Do they go to our school?"

"No."

"How old is Ying?"

"Seventeen."

"How old is Richard?"

"Seventeen."

"How old is Pao?"

"Seventeen."

"And how old are you?"

"Thirteen."

"And where do these boys live?"

"In Minneapolis."

"Where did you meet them?"

"At a funeral."

Hmong funerals are large affairs that last for several days. Many people come, and young people are left to mingle freely for long periods of time.

I ask Mr. Xiong to translate this exchange for Bla's mother. He asks me if he may say something more as well. I nod my approval, and he speaks first to her mother and then directly to Bla, calmly and yet earnestly, almost passionately.

He translates his remarks for me. "I have told her to think about the age difference. Good people age sixteen or seventeen do not make friends with girls so young. She is not mature enough to realize what is going to happen. They may lure her to do bad things."

Now I speak directly to Bla.

"The gangs are always looking for pretty young girls because that is how they make their money. That is what gangsters do. This is a very dangerous business. I don't know if you are playing at being in a gang or if you are in a gang. But I want you to know that gangs are too dangerous to play with. We don't play with fire or loaded guns, and we don't play with gangs either. We have families at our school whose children have been shot and killed by gangs, and we have families who have children in prison because of gangs, and we have families who have had to move to a different house to be safe from gangs, and we have families whose daughters have been kept by gangs. It happens all the time." I go on to state that Bla should not be talking to these boys. That her mother should answer the phone and screen the calls.

Mr. Xiong interprets and then Bla's mother speaks. She is very emotional and struggles to keep her composure.

Mr. Xiong tells me that "regarding the phone situation, they always fight about the phone. Mom answers the phone, but Bla will run and slap her mother's hand. Her mother has told Bla that she has no education because her parents did not let her go to school. She doesn't want her children to struggle and suffer the way she has. She wants them to be educated. She wants Bla to graduate from high school. Then after that, when she is eighteen, she can get married if that is what she wants. Mom is very upset that Bla continues to do this."

Once again I address Bla directly. "What do you think these boys see when they look at you?" She shrugs. "They see a very beautiful young girl. And they want you very badly. But they want you the way the lion wants a lamb. They want you not because they care about you. They do not care about you at all. They want you for what they can get from you. When they look at you they see money. You are valuable to them. Gangs sell young girls for sex. They can make one hundred, maybe two hundred dollars every time you have sex with someone. They use the money to buy expensive cars and drugs. It is their business and they are very good at it. They tell you you are pretty and that they really like you and want to be with you. They ask you to go with them in the middle of the night. They tell you that your parents are old and stupid. They will offer you drugs and have sex with you, and then if you don't want to do it anymore, they will threaten you and your family. They take girls and put them in the trunks of cars and lock them in hotel rooms for days and weeks and sell them to men for sex."

Bla is listening intently.

"I am telling you this because it is the truth and because I care about you. All of us, your mother, your teachers, Mr. Xiong, we all care about you. If you were to become ill, who would be there for you? Who would take care of you?"

"My mother."

"That's right."

I ask Mr. Xiong to interpret for Bla's mother, and once again she offers an emotional response.

Mr. Xiong interprets. "She says that since Bla has been talking to these boys her behavior has changed. She is a good girl, loves her mom and is helpful to her mom, but now she is on the phone all the time. She won't listen to her mom. These boys are asking for directions to her house. They want to come for her late at night, at midnight."

We turn our attention to the contract. It is titled Contract for Resolution of Violations of the Code of Caring Behaviors. Under Recommendations, we agree that Bla and her parents will attend the meeting next Tuesday at 6:00 P.M. We then turn to the section titled Measurable Goals. This section will be up to Bla.

I address her directly. "What do you want your goals to be?"

Without hesitation she offers her goals. We discuss them one at a time for clarification and finally the goals are written and signed:

+ Bla will block the numbers so the boys can't call her house.

+ Bla will tell the boys that she doesn't want to talk to them anymore.

+ If the boys continue to bother Bla, she will tell her parents or Ms. Heisenfelt.

We agree to a follow-up meeting after spring break. It was during spring break just two years ago that another student, Ka Lee, disappeared. She was found two weeks later in a motel room where she was being kept and abused by members of a Hmong gang. The next two weeks will be a critical time. Lions do not give up the hunt easily.

On Tuesday, I meet with Tim and Molly to review our plan for the parent meeting that has been scheduled. To my delight, Molly has brought a packet of excellent information to share with parents at the meeting. These are resources that she has received from Kevin Navara: three pages listing all of the Hmong and Asian gangs and the initials that identify them; information telling parents what to look for if they suspect gang involvement; lists of things that parents can do to help ensure that their children won't join gangs.

We are not sure how to handle this meeting. It seems important that we divide the parents and students for a portion of the time so that the girls will be free to express their ideas and feelings. Molly will facilitate their discussion. We have asked Lee Her to assist her. Lee is a special education paraprofessional and coaches our girls' volleyball team. He will offer effective support.

We agree to add gang activity to the list of Major Violations in the Family Handbook. We also make a list defining what exactly we mean by gang activity:

- Writing things such as gang graffiti, gang names, gang threats, gang statements on anything, anywhere, anytime.

- Talking about anything related to gangs.

- Gang-related threats of any kind.

- Wearing anything that might be gang related, such as colors, belts, hats, shoes, rags, etc. To avoid all suspicion of gang affiliation, be in uniform.

- Using gang-related hand signs.

- Wearing a tattoo or drawing tattoos on one's hands or body.

+ Fights related to gang affiliation.

+ Truancy related to gang affiliation.

Our conversation naturally turns to consequences for violations. All of us agree that they should be restorative. A first violation will require a paper on the subject of gangs and eight hours of verified community service. A second violation, will involve reading the autobiography of a person who made a positive contribution to society and sixteen hours of verified community service. After much discussion, we decide that a third violation would result in expulsion for the remainder of the school year, in accordance with Minnesota's Pupil Fair Dismissal Act.

We will present these consequences at the meeting. At the conclusion of the meeting, we will ask that parents formulate a statement to their daughters and that the girls formulate a statement to their parents. We speculate that this activity will help improve parent–student communication around this important issue.

At 5:45 P.M., Molly stops by my office to inform me that parents are arriving. I head for the library carrying an agenda and a packet of information for each parent, including our policy and consequences, our list of gang-related activities and the information that Kevin Navara has provided. As we begin distributing these written materials, I become painfully aware of the large number of parents present who neither speak nor read English. Our well-prepared handouts will be of no use to them. After so many years, it is still difficult to always remember this!

I keep my opening comments brief and Mr. Xiong interprets. After reviewing the agenda, the girls follow Molly and Lee to the music room, where their meeting will be held.

As I look around the room, I find it of interest that with one exception, all of the parents present are women. Some appear to be in their thirties, and some appear to be in their fifties. One is a professional person who works for an agency that supports parents concerning gang-related issues. A few speak English, but most do not. I suggest that the parents introduce themselves. Some appear to be very shy, but all comply with my request. Mr. Xiong interprets a parent's comment for me. "They would like to have the girls introduce their parents to everyone when they come back so that the parents can know which parents and which girls go together." We agree to follow this wise suggestion.

At this point, I turn the meeting over to Mr. Xiong, and the conversation flows freely. The parents talk about their concerns for their daughters and their frustrations. Much of the conversation concerns rules and limits: What is fair and appropriate? Should the girls be able to talk on the phone? What is a reasonable curfew? Seven o'clock comes and goes and there is no sign of the girls returning. Finally, at 7:50, I decide to interrupt the discussion to encourage the parents to formulate a message to their daughters. As they offer suggestions, Mr. Xiong interprets for me and I write their comments on a chart. As I am doing this, I realize that it is meaningless for many of the parents, but I proceed, thinking that the chart will be important in conveying the parents' ideas to the girls and also because, in my dependency upon the written word, I can't think of a more effective way to accomplish the task. With Mr. Xiong interpreting for me, I try, to the best of my ability, to capture the parents' thoughts.

A message to our daughters:

We care about you and we love you. Please stay focused on your education so you can be a good role model for the little ones. We will always support you to get a good education. Maybe someday you can help us learn English. Study to be a good person so that one day your children will learn from you how to be good people. No one else will give you the love and care we give you. Please think about this and choose the things that will help your future. We want you to have a good job and a good home in your future. We want you to have a good and happy life. Please come together to do good things for the community so we can gladly support you. Maybe you could have a Hmong Culture Club after school. Use positive words, not words that put others down. Use good words. If you want to start a Hmong Culture Club, we could help.

When we finish, it is 8:05. I go the music room and find Lee and Molly still in deep discussion with the girls. They are trying to convince them to make a statement that will assure their parents that they will not engage in gang activity again. I decide not to intervene. At 8:15, the girls rejoin the parents. I ask Mr. Xiong to facilitate the girls' introductions of their parents. This proves to be a very positive activity.

Being aware of the lateness of the hour, I intend to proceed to read the parents' message to the girls and to then ask the girls to share their message with the parents. At this point, however, the one father who is present stands and begins to speak earnestly in Hmong. His speech is followed by another and then another. The meeting has taken on a life of its own. I go to where Lee is standing and ask him to interpret for me. He explains that the parents are talking to the girls. Lee tells me that he and Molly do not want the girls' message to their parents to be overlooked.

After a few more minutes, I go to the front and tell Mr. Xiong that I would like to read the parents' message to the girls and then let the girls share their message with their parents. As I read the parents' message to the girls, it occurs to me that the parents have most probably just conveyed their messages in the way that makes sense to them: orally.

Now Lee Her comes forward with the charts that convey the girls' message to their parents. One of the charts lists the girls' comments regarding gangs:

Gang activity: Get out while you can.
Not worth it . . . sleep on floor . . . don't try it.

Get jumped out when in.
Get tracked down/killed.
Lose trust with parents.
Thought it was cool . . . it's not.
Once you screw up, you can't turn back.
You have the power to be what you want to be.
You are role model for your siblings.
You don't know what guys will do . . . dangerous.

Lee chooses not to share this chart, but moves on the next one. He tries to convey the girls' messages fairly:

The girls feel wrongly accused. They feel like parents assume they are in a gang when they see a group of kids together. Some of the girls feel pushed to go to this school when they would rather go to a different school. They think that in a bigger school, they would have more freedom to choose friends, teachers, classes, and more challenging subjects. Parents have to understand that the girls need a chance to make other choices. They feel that parents expect too much . . . they expect perfection. They think that parents are too strict and that is why some of the girls rebel. They want you to know that they are not going to turn out like their brothers and sisters. The girls said that parents want them to fulfill the dreams they couldn't fulfill in Laos. Also, they want you parents to know that they will put this gang behavior behind them and try their best to avoid gang involvement.

He looks at the girls and asks if he has adequately expressed their ideas to their parents. The girls nod approval. I move to the back of the room during this report. I am not sure what will happen next, but I decide that it is best that I do not interfere in any way.

Again, the parents begin to speak. Some speak in Hmong and some in English. This allows me to follow the gist of the conversation. The parents tell the girls that they are older and wiser. If the girls want to be trusted, then they must be honest and not tell lies.

When they lie to their parents many times, it is difficult to trust. The parents state that they want the girls to go to a school where people know them and care about them. They want them to go to a school where they will get attention and where they will be good students. Parents are older and know what is best.

Mr. Xiong makes concluding remarks. The meeting ends at 8:45 P.M. As the parents file out, several stop to shake my hand and thank me. Those who speak English tell me that they will do anything they can to help.

When all have gone, the staff gathers to debrief. Molly and Lee are somewhat unsettled. They express concern that Hmong parents are often too strict. They say that their meeting with the girls was intense. The girls did some significant sharing. They will probably need to meet with Molly again in the future. All agree that the parents seemed positive and appreciative and that it has been an important evening.

When Mr. Xiong and I reach our offices, we are still talking. I remark that I was proud of the parents for taking a firm stand at the conclusion of the meeting. He says, "The last thing I told the parents was that they do not have to feel embarrassed or ashamed about this meeting. For Hmong parents, these meetings mean embarrassment and shame. Back in Laos, when a child misbehaved the teacher had full authority to discipline, including corporal punishment. Only good news and good reports went home to the parents. Also, parents feel that they are undereducated and do not know how to help their children. They expect the school to take care of everything. At Community of Peace Academy, every time a Hmong parent is called to a behavior meeting, I see the embarrassment in their eyes. I always tell them not to feel embarrassed. I tell them that the meetings are meant to inform them so that all of us can work together to help their child."

I remark that when we include parents in these meetings, we do it to honor them. We see them as the most important person at the meeting because they know their child best. We see them as our equal partner in their child's education, and we honor them and respect them and hold them in high regard.

"Isn't it sad and interesting that what we mean as honor, instead causes embarrassment. It is so difficult! Everything is so different, isn't it?" My comment is offered reflectively, ironically, wistfully. Mr. Xiong laughs his hearty laugh and his eyes twinkle. "Everything!" he exclaims. "Everything!"

EPILOGUE

On October 9–11, 2005, the *Star Tribune* published a special report titled "Shamed into Silence." Written by Pam Louwagie and Dan Browning, the three-part series reported that a subculture of gang rape and prostitution of Hmong girls thrives in the Twin Cities.

> She struggles in the cold grass, sobbing and punching the boy who lay on top of her, but nothing made him stop. She was only 12 years old, and she didn't want to be a bad girl. "No, don't do it," she remembers begging him. "I wanna go home." She had headed to a barbecue with friends earlier that night, but somehow they got separated. She ended up in a St. Paul park with five boys she barely knew.
>
> There in the dark, one of the boys yanked down her blue jeans before dropping his own baggy pants to his knees. He raped her while the others stood nearby, waiting their turn. When the last boy had finished, she pulled her clothes back on, humiliated, exhausted, hurting. But even more devastating to her than the attack was the realization that it might ruin her life.

According to this report, girls as young as twelve are routinely abused in this way, and rape cases of Hmong girls can be especially hard to prosecute. Cultural misunderstanding and fear shame these children into silence, thus exacerbating the problem. We are left with the question, "Will new efforts to combat the Hmong rape problem succeed where others have failed?"

Gang activity remains a prevalent threat to the lives of children, particularly children of color and immigrant children, in all large urban areas and in many smaller communities as well. Fueled by ready access to methamphetamine and other street drugs, gang activity is often cruel and inhumane. Those who fall victim are frequently unable to free themselves. As is true in the Hmong community, cultural taboos may shame both victims and their parents into silence. Without substantial support, few parents are able to intervene on behalf of their children. Schools cannot look the other way. Efforts to combat the strong threat that gangs pose must include a serious restructuring of our nation's schools, particularly schools in gang-infested communities. Promoting trust and caring relationships among students, staff, and parents is essential.

PART V

Building Moral Commitments

How do we build up moral commitments?
There is one way that far surpasses all others.
The important social science observation here is that
experiences are more effective teachers than lectures.

AMITAI ETZIONI,
THE SPIRIT OF COMMUNITY

CHAPTER 19

The Dance

We will be collecting CD's from the students. They will label their CD's
With their names and what number wanted to be played.
(CD's must be rated PG-13, absolutely no rated R)

We will be serving Kool-Aid and chips.
The dancing should be appropriate.

⟜

October 7, 1999

It is the end of another whirlwind day. As I sit in my office, alone at last, I am aware of a group of young people talking and laughing at the picnic table directly outside my open window. A cool breeze ruffles the piles of papers on my desk and the late afternoon sun plays off the autumn leaves. One of the girls spots me, and with a smile walks to the window. "Mrs. Rusthoven, we're having a student council meeting, and we wonder if you would have a minute to talk to us." It is Ka ("Kally") Lee. She has recently been elected as president of our new student council.

Last year, we almost lost Kally. Silently, slowly, almost without notice, she was recruited into a gang. Had it not been for the vigilance and tireless efforts of her teacher and our social worker we might never have known. Her rescue and recovery and her return to youthful innocence are nearly miraculous. I am reminded of my words to Kally as she boarded the school bus on the day before spring break. I held her face in my hands, looked into her eyes, and said, "Please remember how precious you are to all of us." The police found her in a hotel room two weeks later, where she was being kept by the gang. Her shining eyes, her beautiful spirit, and her effective leadership are even more precious to me now.

Kally asked me yesterday if she could meet to talk with me about their plans. The sunshine and the smiling faces are appealing after a long day. I grab a tablet and a pen and head out the door. The students make a place for me at the crowded table. They are seventh, eighth, and ninth graders, recently elected by their peers.

As I settle in, I realize that the students are meeting here after school hours without an adult present.

"Do you have an advisor for the student council?"

"What do you mean?"

"Is there a teacher who meets with you?"

"No. We've decided to meet on Tuesday and Thursday after school. We all have rides or we can walk home."

After I assure myself that they will all be able to find a way home, I make a note to talk with the teachers about this and we proceed.

Kally presents me with a copy of their plans for a Halloween party. She pulls it out of a well-organized notebook. It is an impressive document, and I am pleased.

Kally reviews the plan with me, and I make a few suggestions; the students nod their approval. As I look around the table, a sense of peace comes over me. This is a moment to be savored. I am proud of all of them, and I want them to know it. "I am truly impressed! You have done excellent work here!" They seem pleased.

Paomee remarks, "Well, you know, Mrs. Rusthoven, we *have* been at Community of Peace for four years!"

"Can we have the party?" Kally asks.

"Yes. I think it sounds wonderful."

Her face breaks into a beautiful smile. "Oh, I am so happy! I am so happy!" There are smiles all around. We discuss details, and I

HALLOWEEN PARTY

This is a fund-raising party dance.
$3.00 per person

This is a costume party dance.
If you don't wear a costume we will charge .25 cents.

Costumes must be appropriate.
(Absolutely no weapons or profanity).

Party starts at 6 p.m. and doors close at 7 p.m.
No more entrance after 7 p.m.
The party will end at 10 p.m.

7, 8 and 9 grade students could bring one friend outside of school
to the dance. Before he/she outside of school could get in on the day of
the dance he/she must have their 7, 8, or 9 grade friend sign them up one
day before the dance. The outsider may not be over 16 years of age.

We will need at least two parent and two teacher chaperones at the party.

We will be collecting CD's from the students. They will label their CD's
With their names and what number wanted to be played.
(CD's must be rated PG-13, absolutely no rated R)

We will be serving Kool-Aid and chips.
The dancing should be appropriate.

write a few notes before saying good-bye. I watch from my office as the meeting comes to a close.

At Community of Peace Academy our desired outcome is to educate the whole person—mind, body, and will—for fullness of life. These young people are our first fruits. Their plan for a Halloween party is no small thing. It is evidence of positive will formation. They are making positive decisions and choices, of their own free will, and it is bringing them great joy: another step toward fullness of life.

EPILOGUE

On February 28, 2001, *Education Week* featured a front-page story titled "Freak Dancing" Craze Generates Friction, Fears. To quote: "As the hip hop pounds, the hips intermix; they're 14, 15, 16 year-old hips. They're boys' hips, girls' hips, front to front, back to front. It's twos, it's threes; standing up, bending over. It looks like sex, but it's dancing. Its called freak dancing, and teenagers of all types are freaking at middle and high schools across the country."

The article continues: "At some schools, blanched administrators say, a girl might be on all fours, with one boys' pelvis pressed into her face and another's pressed into her bottom. They see boys on their backs with girls spread-eagled over them; girls bent forward with boys' hips thrust into their back sides. They do it to hip hop and rap. Articles of clothing sometimes come off." The article debated the appropriateness of freak dancing and asked, "Where's the line?"

Our ambivalence on such issues is harmful to our children. Any adult who can remember what it was like to be an adolescent would not question the damage that such dancing could do mentally, physically, spiritually, and emotionally to its young participants. When students are provided positive role models, trusting relationships are fostered, and student leadership is encouraged, students themselves are empowered and inspired to draw the line. This is the path to lives that are whole and full.

CHAPTER 20

Doing What Is Right

Tim tells the boys that his objective was not to have them out of the game. He continues: "Right now the game isn't the issue. What bothers me is that you boys have gone to others with your concerns and at no time have you come to me to acknowledge the situation. At no time did you approach me to resolve this. This would have been a good opportunity to notice and right a wrong. Maybe you didn't think you did anything wrong." Chris says that he doesn't think they did anything wrong.

———

March 2, 2001

It has been a study day for me; a Friday away from school for the purpose of working on my research. For once, I have actually been able to spend the major portion of the day on task with few outside distractions. It is 4:30 p.m. when the phone rings. It is Lou Trudeau, our assistant principal. He is calling to report an incident involving two of the tenth-grade boys. Since I normally handle discipline at the high school, he needs to inform me. What I hear is not good news. Chue Vang and Chris Lo have lost their privilege to play in the championship basketball game on Monday.

It is difficult for me to contain my disappointment. This team has been a real point of pride for the school. As the only Hmong team in the charter school conference, they have taken people by surprise. According to their coach, Aaron Benner, and others who have attended their games, they have been an example of good sportsmanship and respectful behavior in a league where such attributes have been in short supply. It has been my contention that both skill in playing basketball and good character have brought them to this opportunity to play for the championship on Monday night.

Lou tells me that Chue and Chris had been asked by Tim McGowan on Thursday to tuck in their uniform shirts. This is not an uncommon occurrence. Apparently, they complied but soon were seen with their shirts hanging out again. As a result, Tim asked them to come to see him at 3:00. They agreed, but then did not show up. Tim wrote this up as a serious violation, and the conclusion was drawn that they not be allowed to play in the game on Monday as a consequence.

On Saturday morning, I call Eric Fleming. Eric is Chue and Chris's advisor, and I need to get his impression of all of this. I state my concerns. This is not a major violation. What does our policy say? Does it state that a serious violation is grounds for suspension from a game? How does he think Chris and Chue will take this? Will it help them to see the error of their ways, or will it only make them angry and less compliant in the future? Might there be a better way to handle the violation? Eric tells me that he has talked to Tim and that he talked to Chris and Chue at length at the end of the day on Friday. Apparently, the uniform issue has been an ongoing problem with both boys. Many people have asked them repeatedly to tuck in their shirts. Their behavior with Tim was intentionally disrespectful. Eric has made all of this clear to them. On the basis of all of this, he feels that we should stand by the decision to suspend them from the game. He feels that it would send a bad message to all of the kids if we changed our minds.

At the conclusion of our conversation, I am somewhat at peace. It is my primary concern that the boys understand and accept, at least at some level, that this was a fair consequence. Eric and I discuss the fact that our decision underscores the reality of being part of a community. We don't always get to do exactly what we want to do. There are rules. Sometimes, we have to put our own desires aside for the benefit of the team or the community. Hopefully, Chris and Chue will understand this principle and grow from this experience.

I express my sadness one last time. Everyone has worked so hard to get to the championship game. We have planned a pep rally for Monday afternoon and a bus to carry fans to the game. This casts a cloud over the festivities. Eric assures me that we have done the right thing and that it will still be fun. Reluctantly, I decide that I must trust and let go of my concern.

On Monday, as I am listening to my messages, my secretary walks in and hands me a note: "Chue Vang and Chris Lo would like to meet with you." I call Tim McGowan and we decide that both of us will meet with the boys during their lunch period. I begin our meeting by asking the boys why they wanted to see me. Chris says, "Because me and Chue really want to play in the championship game." Chue adds, "If the team wins, we don't deserve the reward."

Tim tells the boys that his objective was not to have them out of the game. "Right now," he says, "the game isn't the issue. What bothers me is that you boys have gone to others with your concerns and at no time have you come to me to acknowledge the situation. At no time did you approach me to resolve this. This would have been a good opportunity to notice and right a wrong. Maybe you didn't think you did anything wrong." Chris says that he doesn't think they did anything wrong. I decide that the best thing I can do is to leave Tim and the boys to talk this out. I excuse myself and make my way to the cafeteria.

Later, as I am about to leave the cafeteria to check on Tim and the boys, I see Dan coming toward me. He is our sixth-grade teacher's assistant and coaches the eighth-grade boys' team. He tells me that he is pleased that we followed through on suspending Chris and Chue from the game. Only last week, one of his players was suspended from a playoff game for disrespectful behavior to his coaches. He tells me that even though it was hard, he thinks it was a very good lesson for him. He says he thinks it would have been a big mistake to let them play.

When I get upstairs I find Tim with Chris McElroy, our athletic director. Tim says that the boys came around somewhat in their conversation with him. Chris confirms the athletic policy that states that athletes must follow the code of caring behaviors and that an infraction will result in suspension from the team for one week or one game. We have followed our policy. All of us agree that the fact that the championship game is affected is truly unfortunate. Later I find an e-mail from Eric stating that he has heard rumors of further negotiations going on regarding the boys' suspension from the game and stating his strong opposition to any thought of overturning the decision. I send an e-mail assuring him that the decision stands.

The pep rally is lively, and Chris and Chue sit on the stage with the team. I am both pleased and sad to see them there. At 5:30 P.M. my husband arrives with the bus. He drives for all of our games and has kept me informed on how well the team has been playing. This will be only the second game I have attended this season. With the exception of my husband and Danny's parents, our team has rarely had fans at their games. For this special occasion, we have made an effort to ensure that our team will have fans in the stands.

Our team plays in a new league that was created last year for charter schools, and since none of the schools have regulation-size gyms, all of the games are played at the Boys and Girls Club.

A number of students have brought permission slips and two dollars for a membership card to the Boys and Girls Club and are riding the bus with the team. Chris McElroy rides the bus as well. My dad and my son and his wife are planning to meet us at the game. Several teachers show up to offer their support. Spirits are high.

The team we are playing today has beaten us before. All of their players are African American. Aaron Benner, our coach, is African American, but all of our players, except for Danny, are Hmong, and Danny is Hispanic. The other team's players tend to be intimidating and disrespectful. Aaron has expressed his concern about this team before.

During warm-ups our opponents have thirteen players on the floor. Without Chue and Chris, we have seven players. Later, I notice that Vang is sitting on the bench as well, and I learn that at the last minute, he was also suspended from the game for academic reasons. We are down to six players.

Aaron calls it to the attention of the officials that a number of the players on the other team were not on the team the last time we played them. Unfortunately, this team has gained a poor reputation in the league. The officials check the roster and eliminate four of their players from the game. The game begins.

As the game progresses, it becomes apparent that our opponents are angry and intend to win at all costs. Their coach is encouraging this, and they are in a frenzy. Tensions mount. Throughout the game, our six players remain calm. At no time do they become angry or confrontational. I am amazed at their ability to maintain their composure under this repeated negative pressure. Our opponents are given one, then a second, and then a third technical foul. Finally with two seconds left, the game is called. We have won by two points. Our opponents erupt in fury.

At this point, my son, who coaches high school basketball in Minneapolis, and Aaron and Chris, are truly concerned about the safety of our players and fans. We are held in the gym, and the other team is escorted out. When we are ready to leave, we learn that several of their players are outside waiting for us and will not leave. The police are called. Nearly twenty minutes later, the police arrive, and we are given an escort to our bus. Aaron is visibly upset. As we wait for the police, he says to no one in particular, "Welcome to the real world."

The next day Mr. McElroy tells me that he has officially reported our concerns regarding the game and that the league has assured him that they would follow up on it. Mr. Benner reports that he called the principal of our opponent's school and that the principal had supported the actions of their coach. He is baffled by this response and advises me not to do anything more.

When I see Chris and Chue in the cafeteria the following day, I make it a point to talk to each one of them individually. I attempt to make the point that the game was a classic example of what matters and what doesn't matter. The other team lost, but not because they had no talent. They had plenty of talent. They lost because they lacked character. Their behavior was so unethical that they lost the game. My timing is not good. Both boys seem unforgiving and impatient for me to stop. Hopefully, someday, they will understand.

EPILOGUE

On June 11, 2003, Chris Lo delivered the following speech at his graduation ceremony:

> *I would like to start off by thanking Ms. Nyholm and Mr. Fleming for letting me speak today at graduation. It is an honor and a privilege to have a moment like this. It will follow me always.*
>
> *I remember the first day I set foot in Community of Peace Academy. When I began school here four years ago, it was an experience for me. I mean, how many times in your life have you walked into a school and had everyone smiling at you; every single person. I never did until the first day at CPA. When I was in class for the first time, we all got into what we call Peace Circle and that was when I was introduced to my classmates with every one of them smiling. Scary huh? It was*

like, "Hi, I'm Chue," and then a big smile. "Hi, I'm Mary," and then a smile. The smiling wasn't at all odd or scary, it was rather welcoming. But, it was not just all the smiling and happiness that made me want to be here at CPA.

I believe it was because of one particular person at this school that I wanted to be here. It was my first high school teacher, Mr. Fleming. It was kind of funny because he looked like my favorite fighting character from a video game I used to play back then. Mr. Fleming was about two and a half feet taller than me and I thought he had some great kung fu skills in him and that he could obviously dunk. When I met Mr. Fleming it was hilarious. Dr. Rusthoven said, "You have a new student today. His name is Chris Lo and he's from California." Mr. Fleming turned around with this really big smile and gave me this big ol' whopping monstrous handshake that made me wish my arm and hand could be amputated at that moment in time. But, don't get me wrong. That handshake that he gave me wasn't at all painful or hurtful to me. Instead, it opened my eyes and I saw what great friendships these people had. It made me feel like I belonged, and in that very moment, I knew that Community of Peace Academy would be the place where I was going to grow up and that it was going to be my new home.

It's weird how friends become good friends and good friends become best friends and then, before you know it, you're one great big family. Your classmates become your brothers and sisters and your teachers become your parents. I will always remember the laughter and happiness that we shared together on our school field trips and especially in our classrooms. As a group, we all grew up, and as a group, we all grew up strong. To all my classmates, I thank you for this strength.

So before I finish my speech, I would like to give thanks to all the teachers and staff who pushed me and helped me receive this incredible gift. To my classmates, the class of 2003, I love *you guys. I wouldn't have made it with out all of you too. I hope you achieve all your goals in life and beat any obstacles that stand in your way. I wish you all the best. Thank you!*

It is not easy to teach ethical and moral behavior amidst the pressures of our prevailing culture. Community of Peace Academy is attempting to educate for fullness of life for all. This new vision requires that everyone embrace high ethical and moral standards. It calls for moral excellence that is demanding, somewhat counter cultural and often painful to achieve. Yet the ultimate rewards are priceless. Chris captured the essence of this important work in his graduation speech:

It's weird how friends become good friends and good friends become best friends and then, before you know it, your one great big family. Your classmates become your brothers and sisters and your teachers become your parents. I will always remember the laughter and happiness that we shared together on our school field trips and especially in our classrooms. As a group, we all grew up, and as a group, we all grew up strong.

In the end, moral strength cannot be imposed upon anyone. Each person will accept or reject it of his or her own free will, and in his or her own time. The best we can do is to lead by example and to remain strong in our resolve, even under pressure.

CHAPTER 21

The Power of Art

As the right panel of the mural is completed, my emotional attachment to it continues to grow. It reminds me of Benjamin's personal struggle to find fullness of life. Like the young man in the painting, Benjamin is rooted. He has a faith and he has a loving heart. Clearly, the young man in our mural, rooted to the earth and reaching with his whole body for the star, symbolizes hope. As long as there is life, there is hope.

➤

March 2001

For the past five and one-half weeks a mural of incredible scope has been taking shape in our school library. The first seeds of this momentous endeavor were planted in October of 1999, when I first met Deborah Boldt, national director of the Fresco Community Outreach Program. This amazing program grew out of the production of Deborah's film *Fresco*, which documents the creation of the fresco, commissioned by the University of St. Thomas, to adorn the ceiling of its school of education in downtown Minneapolis. The St. Thomas fresco, created by Mark Balma, depicts the seven virtues of St. Thomas Aquinas. The Fresco Community Outreach Program provides resident artists to work with students, to assist them in creating their own visual interpretations of the values that are held within their schools or communities. When we learned that students had created several public murals throughout the

Twin Cities area, it became apparent that this program was a perfect fit for Community of Peace Academy.

In October of 1999, a new addition to the facilities at Community of Peace Academy was nearing completion. This addition included a library/meeting room. The focal point of this lovely space was a circular bank of ceiling-to-floor windows framed by two large side panels. The windows highlighted a raised circular gathering space. As I stood one day admiring this unique space, it suddenly occurred to me that this would be the place for our mural. We would not rest until the walls and circular ceiling of our library were adorned with our students' own interpretations of the ethical principles upon which the school was founded. On February 5, 2001, nearly seventeen months later, the mural residency began at Community of Peace Academy.

Now it is March and our library looks as though it is once again under construction. White butcher paper has been hung ceiling to floor to partition off the entire area where the tenth-grade class and resident artists work. The students arrive in groups of five or ten throughout each day. Marilyn Lindstrom and Gustavo Lira are artistic directors, and Neng Lee is artistic and cultural mentor. All three are accomplished artist and muralists.

The project has not been without its challenges: The staff needed to adjust to the limited space in the library during the six-week residency, and student use of the space has been somewhat limited. In the third week, the student artists began to complain that they were not being listened to regarding which drawings should become part of the mural. A special meeting was called to hear and address their concerns. The project was slightly behind schedule because, among other things, it took an entire day to adequately cover the carpeting on the circular stairs and platform under the circular ceiling that would become part of the mural.

I visit the library as often as possible to view the work as it takes shape. The floor in the work area is completely covered by taped-together cardboard. Two tables are covered with an organized mess of odd containers of paint. Countless drawings are taped to the white strips of butcher paper that hang from ceiling to floor. Other tables are covered with pictures and books that have been used as references. The students' drawings are remarkable.

Two sets of scaffolding have been placed in the raised circular area where the ceiling will be painted. Drawings selected for the mural are enlarged and then carefully transferred to the ceiling and walls. Pictures are transferred to the ceiling through a complex process that involves perforating the lines of each drawing, attaching them to the ceiling and then "pouncing them" with chalk. In order to draw and paint on the ceiling, students must often lie on their backs on top of the scaffolding.

The ceiling panel is the first to take shape. In the center of the circular ceiling is the earth as seen from space. Four hands of different skin tones hold the earth in place. This image is outlined by three doves. As soft colors are added and delicately blended, the images convey a sense of peace and beauty.

This circular ceiling is surrounded by a flat circular frame about two and one-half feet wide; the frame has always been there, but had until now escaped my notice. As the mural takes shape, it becomes apparent that the artists will include this circular frame in the mural. I am perplexed to see two strong images taking shape in this framed area: a dragon and a tiger. They are beautiful, but, with their claws and watchful eyes, they seem to create a stark contrast to the soft peaceful scene in the center. I find this somewhat unsettling and so I ask Marilyn the meaning of the dragon and the tiger. I am told that the tiger is a symbol of courage and that the dragon symbolizes imagination. So be it. I will learn to live with it.

Next, drawings are transferred to the panel on the left. Kalia Thao's drawing of justice is the focus of this panel. Her picture received many votes from the students. Kalia has drawn a woman with dark flowing hair; she is draped in a long garment that drops from her shoulders, exposing her bare breasts. She is carrying the scale of justice and is surrounded by a frame of ribbon. As soon as the drawing is on the wall, Marilyn Lindstrom calls to ask me if I think the breasts should be covered. She thinks this would be most appropriate, but Gustavo is in favor of leaving the drawing as it is. I decide to let them work it out as they see fit. Before the day ends, I have received several complaints from lower-grade teachers and it is decided that the breasts will be covered.

The right panel remains empty for several days. When a drawing is finally agreed upon for this panel, I am delighted to see that it is one I had especially admired. It is Chue Vang's drawing of a man, kneeling on the ground with arms outstretched as he points to a star. For several more days, he has no face. It is finally decided that justice will have an Asian face and that the kneeling figure will be African American, representing the two predominant groups at Community of Peace Academy.

When the face appears, I can't help but notice a strong resemblance to my son, Benjamin. This is not my imagination and it gives me something to think about. As more detail is added, the figure is shown to be rooted to the earth. A heart is painted just to his left and a rose grows from the heart—images of love. After much deliberation, it is decided that to complete this panel an angel will be added. She will be just above his head on the right: a symbol of faith. This work tugs at my heart.

On March 6, the morning headlines tell of yet another school shooting. This time, a fifteen-year-old boy, a tenth-grade student in Santee, California, has shot and killed two students and wounded thirteen in what is reported as the deadliest school shooting since the one in Columbine. The story reports that the boy attended a school of 1,900 and was routinely picked on by other students. A classmate described him as the subject of constant harassment.

On my way to school that morning, I think and pray. From kindergarten on, we teach the children to give up putdowns and to praise people. We teach them to seek wise people when they need assistance and to notice and speak up about hurts they cause and to right wrongs. Even in our school of 420 students it takes a total commitment from everyone every day to maintain a caring, safe, and peaceful environment for our students. The work is not easy, but it is so vitally, urgently important.

During my morning visit to the library, Marilyn Lindstrom is excited to show me something she has received from Yoon Kee Tan. Yoon Kee teaches ESL and is from Singapore. She has given Marilyn a paper describing the meaning of the dragon in Chinese tradition. According to the new information, the dragon is also a symbol of courage.

As I look overhead at the watchful dragon and tiger guarding the soft pastel images of unity and peace, all at once, everything comes into focus. There is no easy path to peace. It is a precious and elusive goal. Only those with the courage, strength, and tenacity of dragons and tigers will ever see their dreams of peace fulfilled. I am reminded of the great men and women who have worked to bring peace and justice to our world: Nelson Mandela, Martin Luther King Jr., Mohandas Gandhi, Mother Teresa, Harriet Tubman, Archbishop Romero—these were dragons and tigers for peace. Peace work is not for the faint of heart.

In the fifth week, the mural is nearing completion, and the time has come to name it. As I stand looking at this work that has come to mean so much to me, I am struck by the fact that I am beholding a visualization of fullness of life for all. This is what it means. The students have captured it. When I discuss this idea with them, they graciously consent to name the mural *Fullness of Life for All*.

As the right panel of the mural is completed, my emotional attachment to it continues to grow. It reminds me of Benjamin's personal struggle to find fullness of life. Like the young man in the painting, Benjamin is rooted. He has a faith and he has a loving heart. Clearly, the young man in our mural, rooted to the earth and reaching with his whole body for the star, symbolizes hope. As long as there is life there is hope.

The day before we must order the plaque that will officially name the mural for posterity, I am still reflecting on these things.

I think of the student artists and their own personal struggles. Every day, each of us is confronted with choices and decisions that will lead us to fullness of life or not. This is a lifelong struggle that will require courage, hope, love, and faith. Fullness of life for all is never a given. It is always an elusive challenge. I propose a new name: *The Challenge: Fullness of Life for All*. With understanding, the students accept the amendment.

March 29, the day before spring break, proves to be an incredible day at Community of Peace Academy. In spite of the fact that we have conferences that evening, we have scheduled the dedication of our mural for 5:00 P.M. to accommodate Deborah Boldt's schedule. In addition to all of this, my birthday, which is on Sunday, is being celebrated that day, and so my day is punctuated by unexpected hugs, songs, and surprise greetings.

Most of our energy throughout the day is directed toward getting ready for the mural celebration. Deborah and Marilyn Lindstrom arrive early and have been in the library all day making preparations. With the assistance of the tenth-grade students, they have sorted and hung all of the students' original drawings that were a part of the six-week residency that created the mural we will dedicate tonight.

Ten of the drawings that appear in the mural have been framed and will be permanently hung in the library. In addition to Kalia Thao's drawing of justice and Chue Vang's visualization of hope, they include Chue Vang and Chris Lo's circular drawing of the dragon and tiger, Long Kue's angel and doves, and Chai Yang's rose springing up from a heart.

The ninth-grade class has been working throughout the past six weeks to create original musical interpretations of the virtues for our celebration this evening. The Orff instruments that will be used are brought in and set up in the circular area beneath the mural's circular ceiling panel. Chairs are arranged, the sound system is put in place, and rehearsals are held throughout the day.

Deborah, Marilyn, and Eric Fleming put final touches on the program. Student certificates are printed and signed and flowers are delivered. Eric's car has lost its brakes, so he borrows mine to pick up the cake and groceries for the reception.

As the five o'clock hour approaches, Eric and his wife prepare the reception in the faculty lounge. I give final thought to my brief remarks. I have invited my father, and when he arrives at 4:45, I am amazed that it is already nearly time for the program to begin. I finish my notes and we head for the library. Parents are arriving for conferences. The school is alive with activity.

And there, under the lights, the mural is a radiant presence: the main attraction and guest of honor for the evening's celebration. This night will feature our high school students: the ninth-grade musicians and the tenth-grade artists. I will keep my remarks brief. Each of the student and resident artists is given a rose as he or she arrives. The library is filled with admiring guests and supporters when we begin at 5:08 P.M.

It is a joyful event. The students' musical compositions are impressive and moving. The mural speaks for itself, filling the room with new warmth and meaning. The artists are introduced and honored with bouquets of roses. The student artists explain the process they followed throughout the residency, and slides of the process are shown. As the tenth graders come up to receive their certificates of achievement, I thank each one personally. When all have been recognized and are assembled, I make my closing statement:

> *The resident artists, student artists and all who have contributed to this project have given our community a gift that we will always cherish. As principal of Community of Peace Academy, I want to express my gratitude for their gift. However, on a more personal note, I want to tell you that your artwork, has touched my soul and my spirit. I do not have time this evening to go into great detail about my own personal experience of your work, but it has great meaning for me personally.*

This is the purpose of art. At its best, true art has the power to touch the human soul. There is no higher compliment I can give you.

As I begin to thank and dismiss our guests to the reception, Marilyn stops me and says that Sammy has something to say. I step aside and Sammy comes forward to the microphone. He, not I, will have the final word. "I want to say thank you to the artists, Marilyn and Gustavo and Neng. And I want to thank Mrs. Rusthoven for giving me this opportunity to touch her soul."

CHAPTER 22

It Takes a Village

The single most memorable experience that I have had from my entire education career was walking through Chinatown while on the eighth grade class trip to Chicago. I remember walking through a street full of surprises: the people, the food, the stores, the restaurants, Chinese stuff, the noises. As a 13 year old Hmong boy leaving Minnesota for the first time, my mind was blown. I realized how big the world was and a curiosity started to grow inside me. It made me want to see and experience new things in life. I'm glad that I came to this school, because it taught me more than just academics.

Each spring since 1999, the eighth-grade class has traveled to Chicago for its class trip. The purpose of this trip is to encourage students to reach beyond their comfort zones in building friendships, to participate in service to others, and to experience a new city and state.

The theme of the trip is "Friendship." Daily themes, which focus on various aspects of friendship, are presented during a morning circle. As students leave the morning circle, they draw names for Secret Pals. Throughout the day, they secretly try to make sure that this person has a happy day. At the close of each day, students sit in a circle, by candlelight, around a basket that contains a token (one for each person) to remind them of the daily theme. Each person writes a Care Card for their Secret Pal. Then, one person picks a token from the basket, presents it to his or her Secret Pal, and reads the Care Card. This ritual is repeated until all have been honored by their Secret Pals.

This special trip has been made possible by the generosity and enthusiasm of many people. Each spring, Itasca Presbyterian Church in Itasca, Illinois, offers the use of their facility for sleeping and their kitchen for meal preparation. Members of the church welcome us with a pizza supper on the evening of our arrival and on occasion, have invited our group to their homes.

Transportation is provided by school buses owned by the school and driven by my husband and Don Dixon, a friend who drives for the MTC and takes his vacation each year in order to help with the class trip.

A highlight of the trip is a potluck picnic provided by parents and enjoyed in a park along the way. This multicultural feast includes such Hmong delicacies as sticky rice, chicken wings, egg rolls and papaya salad, and Eritrean flat bread and a spicy Eritrean mixed vegetable dish.

Each year, First Presbyterian Church on the south side of Chicago, has provided an opportunity for students to be of service to others by welcoming our participation in their outreach ministries. These activities have included working in community gardens, cleaning up trash, sorting donations for a clothing center, and assisting in distributing food and preparing meals for the homeless.

Itineraries have included, among other things, visits to the John Hancock Observatory, Museum of Science and Industry, Shedd Aquarium, Peace Museum, Lincoln Park Zoo, and a walk down Michigan Avenue. A must each year, rain or shine, is dinner and shopping in China Town and a photo shoot at the Buckingham Fountain after dark. The ease with which we have been able to follow our busy and varied itineraries has been due in large part, to the fact that my husband was born and raised in Chicago.

Perhaps most impressive is the generous spirit with which

members of the staff have embraced this trip. Administrators, teachers, paraprofessionals, the school social worker, the home–school liaison, and even a frequent substitute teacher have, with great enthusiasm, chaperoned the "Chicago Trip," riding to Chicago and back on a school bus, sleeping on the floor, and giving up their time to make it happen.

On the trip home, each person on the bus writes a Care Card to every other person. At the closing circle, each student and staff member receives an envelope filled with Care Cards from each person on the bus. In spite of our weariness, there is never a doubt that we will board the bus and head for Chicago again the next year. The letters that follow were written in June of 2001 and express the students' appreciation of this trip.

Dear Ms. Rusthoven,

I'm writing to thank you for letting us go on this trip to Chicago and for helping all of the eighth graders with what ever they need help with. I would also like to thank you for coming up with the secret pals and the topics for the friendship theme. I thought that was great. I really enjoyed the secret pals because it helped me get to know people I don't normally hang out with. I also liked it because I realize I didn't know lots of my class mates like I thought I did.

I would like to thank Mr. Rusthoven also for driving all them hours for us kids. I really appreciated all that everyone did to make it feel like a real experience especially for taking us to that church with all them homeless people. I really took that seriously. I think that's the only thing that I saw in my life and really felt like I was going to cry. Maybe it was because I seen lots of kids there. I don't know, it really hurt me to have to see people who have to live the way they do. When I looked at some of them leaving all I could think was, are they going to a safe place? My favorite thing was going to the zoo and going to see that colorful water fountain. Thank you so much for everything.

Sincerely,
Shaquinta Coleman

—

Dear Ms. Rusthoven,

Thanks for planning the trip to Chicago for us. On the trip I not only had a lot of fun but I learned a lot of things too. One thing I learned was that friendship is a very important and beautiful thing. I saw that after this trip was over the other students in my class changed because they got along better and are also closer to each other.

One impact it had on my life was when we were helping the poor, I felt good about it because it was like I was giving up my free time to help them, and one of them came up to me and praised me for my work which made me feel even better.

When we did the secret pal thing I got Tou Chao, Kiel, Tou Shoua and Mr. McGowan. I learned that if you really look and try to think of something good about somebody you will always find it because everybody has something good about them. Thank you for making this trip possible. This will remain in my memory for the rest of my life.

Sincerely,
Chue Feng Moua

Memories of the eighth-grade class trip endure. Tony Lor, a member of the Community of Peace Academy class of 2005, shared these words during his high school graduation ceremony:

I've been a student at Community of Peace Academy for 10 years. This school has played a big role in my life. It has taught me to read, to write, to add, to subtract, learn how to take tests and how to pass tests. But all schools do this. So much more than that, Community of Peace Academy has taught me to respect, to care, to love, and to build peace.

One way CPA helps students learn these things is by taking trips and doing things outside the classroom. The single most memorable experience that I have had from my entire education career, was walking through Chinatown while on the eighth grade class trip to Chicago.

I remember walking through a street full of surprises: the people, the food, the stores, the restaurants, Chinese stuff, the noises. As a 13 year old Hmong boy leaving Minnesota for the first time, my mind was blown. I realized how big the world was and a curiosity started to grow inside me. It made me want to see and experience new things in life. I'm glad that I came to this school, because it taught me more than just academics.

It is true that it takes a village to raise a child. When many people unselfishly pool their resources and give generously of their time and talents on behalf of children, wonderful things happen. Such experiences have potential to change a child's life permanently for the better.

CHAPTER 23

Vision Quest

Perched high above the frozen waters of the St. Croix is a lodge whose basement witnessed an incredible conversation Thursday evening. A group of us sat in a circle on hard, yellow metal chairs and pondered the immense importance of peace, justice, freedom, compassion, wholeness and fullness of life for all. Students talked of how they wanted to live out CPA's ideology in their lives; they shared their dreams for themselves, for their families and for the world. This, my friends, was a testament to the values each of us practice every day.

In their eleventh-grade year, students at Community of Peace Academy attend a Vision Quest Retreat. This overnight retreat is held at a camp on the St. Croix River. Focusing on the vision of the school, students are encouraged to imagine how this vision may become a reality in their lives.

> The vision of Community of Peace Academy is to educate the whole person—mind, body, and will—for peace, justice, freedom, compassion, wholeness and fullness of life for all.

Students are reminded that wholeness and fullness of life is the final state of one who has consistently made decisions and choices, of his or her own free will, that led to mental, physical, emotional, and spiritual health and well-being for self and others. The content of the retreat is as follows.

PART I

Each of us has a will, or spirit that guides us in all of our decisions and choices. Parents, family members, teachers, and friends can and do offer us guidance and advice. In the end, we must decide what things we will and will not say and do. We must decide who our friends will be, how we will spend our time and what our goals will be.

1. Who are the people in your life right now who are trying to give you guidance and direction regarding your future? Of these people, who are you most likely to listen to, or whose advice are you most likely to follow? Why is this person's advice most meaningful to you?

When we make decisions and choices of our own free will that lead to our own health and well-being, those decisions and choices bring peace and freedom to our spirits. When we make decisions and choices that hurt us, our spirits are often troubled, sad, angry, and confused. We do not feel at peace and we may feel that we are trapped by our bad decisions and choices.

2. When you make decisions and choices that affect your personal mental, physical, emotional or spiritual health, how can you tell if they were good or not so good? Give an example of a decision you have made recently that turned out to be either good for you or not so good for you. If it was not so good a decision, were you able to correct it? If so, how? If not, why not?

When we make decisions and choices of our own free will that lead to the health and well-being of others, those decisions and choices bring justice and compassion to our world. When our

decisions and choices hurt others, we may find ourselves in un-caring and hurtful situations that may lead to violence.

3. Tell about a decision or choice that you made recently that affected someone else either in a good way, or in a not so good way. What were the results of this decision? If the results were not so good, were you able to right the wrong? If so, how? If not, why not?

Everyone longs for peace and freedom of spirit. People often look for peace and freedom for their spirits in all the wrong places. In truth, a spirit that is free and at peace is the reward we get when we make decisions and choices that lead to mental, physical, emotional, and spiritual health and well-being for ourselves and others ... These are the rewards of a truly good life. Please keep this in mind as you work on the questions in Part II.

PART II

Each person is totally unique ... a one of a kind, special creation. Each person has been given special gifts and talents that no one else has been given in quite the same way or at quite the same time in the history of the world.

1. What are some of the unique gifts you have? These can be qualities of character, athletic talents, musical talents, or anything that brings you special happiness or joy. (Don't be shy. If you cannot think of what your special gifts are, ask someone that loves you very much, like your parents, or grandparents or your best friend.)

2. Now think about things that interest you. These may or may not be things that you have been able to experience. Name some things that especially interest you (like designing a building, playing the guitar, flying an airplane, or learning how to cook).

I'm sure that you've heard the saying, "Today is the first day of the rest of your life." This means that no matter what has happened in your life up to this time, today is a new beginning. This is a very important time in your life.

3. What is most important to you at this time in your life? What are your top priorities right now? List up to five. List them from most important to least important.

Imagine yourself five years from now. Five years ago, you were in the sixth grade. That doesn't seem that long ago, does it? Five years from now, you could have graduated from college or trade school. You could be working as a teacher, engineer, architect, electrician, or social worker. You could be married. You could have children. You could be living, studying, or working in another state or another country. You could be studying to be a doctor or a lawyer. You could own your own business or you could be a business manager. You could be doing volunteer work anywhere in the world. The possibilities are endless!

4. When you think about your future, what are some careers that really interest you? List them:

Now circle the one career that, at the moment, seems most interesting to you and share why you might feel this way:

5. What will you need to be doing while you are still in high school so that you will be prepared for the career

that you circled in number 4 above? Think of the priorities that you listed in number 3. Are they going to help to prepare you for this career? If not, how would you need to alter or change your priorities?

6. Now think about your family. How would your family feel about this career choice? Why? How important is it to you to have your family's approval? Could your spirit feel free and at peace without your family's approval?

7. If you are successful in this career, will it help you to find wholeness and fullness of life for yourself? Explain.

8. Think about the impact that your career choice will have upon others. If you are successful in this career, will it help others find wholeness and fullness of life? How will the world become a better place if you are successful in this career?

Each year, members of the staff write letters of support and encouragement to the Vision Quest students. Since Community of Peace Academy serves grades K to 12, many of the teachers have developed caring relationships with these students along the way. Following the 2003 Vision Quest Retreat, the students' advisor, Jon Olson, sent this e-mail to the staff:

Dear Staff,

The 11th grade retreat was a tremendous success! I would like to offer my personal thanks to many of you who wrote letters of support and encouragement to 11th grade students. Your letters showed these students the extraordinary devotion you have toward helping them take control of their futures. I have heard rumors that some of you wrote over seven letters!

Thursday morning students read the letters during the bus ride to Camp St. Croix. As the bus rambled eastward on I-94, I myself reflected on the uniqueness of each of the students and the amazing synergy we have built at Community of Peace. I talked with one student about his letters of support. He lamented that he did not know the authors well. However, as he continued to tell about his letters, it was clear the authors know him. He was shocked at the personal and accurate insight the letters contained. "I can't believe the person who wrote this letter knows me this well," he said.

Perched high above the frozen waters of the St. Croix is a lodge whose basement witnessed an incredible conversation Thursday evening. A group of us sat in a circle on hard, yellow metal chairs and pondered the immense importance of peace, justice, freedom, compassion, wholeness and fullness of life for all. Students talked of how they wanted to live out CPA's ideology in their lives; they shared their dreams for themselves, for their families and for the world. This, my friends, was a testament to the values each of us practice every day. Clearly, these students had learned life lessons from the staff. As we talked, no one was left out, everyone was heard, and the students became adults. No one had to say, "I'm ready for questions and comments." No one had to be encouraged to speak louder or to share. No one left the room without feeling uplifted and confident in their convictions to become the person they dream of being.

You all are tremendous colleagues! I feel lucky to work with you as we push ourselves and our students towards whole and full lives for all. While many of the 11th grade students may not be ready to articulate their thanks, they do sense the distinctiveness of our school and the staff that work with them. Please accept my enthusiastic thanks and congratulations on their behalf.

Jon Olson

CHAPTER 24

One Thousand Cranes

Just as you will remember, so will we. We will work together to end this foolishness called "gangs". If ever asked to join one, we will refuse. Any one of us could have been in Michael's place, and we can't forget that.

In late October 2005, Michael Duong, a thirteen-year-old St. Paul boy, was fighting for his life in Regions Hospital. On October 4, the Ramsey County Attorney's Office charged two seventeen-year-old boys with attempted murder in the first degree for the benefit of a gang in connection with Michael's brutal beating the night of September 23, 2005. On that fateful day, Michael Duong and a friend were visiting in front of a house on the east side of St. Paul, while Michael's father visited the owner inside. Julio Cesar Robles and Miguel Ramirez happened to drive by. In what has been described as an incredibly vicious attack, the two seventeen-year-olds used a baseball bat and beat and kicked Michael to the brink of death because he was wearing a red sweatshirt, the color of an opposing gang. Michael had no gang affiliation.

When students at Community of Peace Academy heard about this brutal beating in their neighborhood, they were saddened and dismayed. Maggie Struck, a paraprofessional at Community of Peace Academy, had just organized an origami club for students in grades 7 and 8. Shepherded by Maggie, students decided to take action on Michael's behalf. What followed was a heartfelt act of hope.

Dear Duong Family,

Hello. My name is Nicole Wagner. I go to Community of Peace Academy, which is a charter school on the east side of Saint Paul. In our school, we learn about peace and ethics along with things like math and science. In our history class, we do Current Events, which is how we first learned about Michael.

We are always hearing about how gangs in our community are getting bigger, and about how they have "gang wars". However, when we heard about a boy, a 13 year old boy, who got hurt from it we finally realized how bad the problem really is. A few of the kids in my class actually used to go to school with Michael, and we got together to create an idea. We wanted to show how much we care about what happened to Michael, and what you must be going through. As his family, you care about him more than any other.

A few years ago, we all read about a Japanese girl named Sadako. In the book, it says that if someone can make 1,000 paper cranes, then they can get a wish. So, in only two days, 200 students in my school made over 1,000 cranes.

We want you to have the wish. With these 1,000 cranes, we will share with you the wish that Michael gets better, and that no other person or family has to go through what you are going through. Know that in these cranes are the hopes of 200 children. All of us want Michael and you to heal from this. You will never forget about it, but the situation will get better.

Just as you will remember, so will we. We will work together to end this foolishness called "gangs". If ever asked to join one, we will refuse. Any one of us could have been in Michael's place, and we can't forget that.

And Michael, when you read this, know that even in a world as confused and war filled as this, you will never truly be alone.

Sincerely,
Nicole Wagner, Junior High Student Council President

We must take time in our school day to respond in positive ways to violent events that occur within the neighborhoods in which our students live. Encouraging and supporting students in reaching out to their neighbors in times of crisis, empowers and inspires them. Through such experiences, they learn that their actions can make a positive difference and that their efforts can improve the world they live in.

The Challenge: Fullness of Life For All

Dedicated: March 29, 2001

This mural was created by the tenth grade class. These students will be the first graduates of Community of Peace Academy. The mural depicts the ethical principles upon which the school was founded:

Caring, Respect, Courage, Justice, Peace, Faith, Hope and Love.

The circular ceiling panel depicts caring and respect of the earth and all her people. The doves encircle the earth as a symbol of world peace. The dragon and tiger encircle the vision of peace with a mantel of courage, strength and imagination without which peace is only a distant dream. The side panels depict the day and the night. On the left a dove hovers above the figure of justice. The lotus is a symbol of life. The right panel depicts man: rooted to earth, yet striving for the stars. This powerful figure, surrounded by faith and love, gives us hope, as we face the challenge to reach our vision of fullness of life for all.

STUDENT ARTISTS

Members of the Class of 2003

ARTISTS IN RESIDENCE

Marilyn Lindstrom ◆ Gustavo Lira ◆ Neng Lee

THIS MURAL IS A JOINT PROJECT OF
COMMUNITY OF PEACE ACADEMY AND THE
FRESCO COMMUNITY OUTREACH PROGRAM

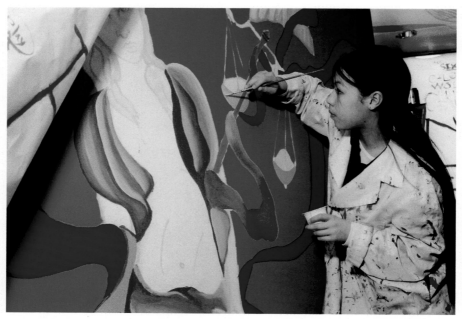

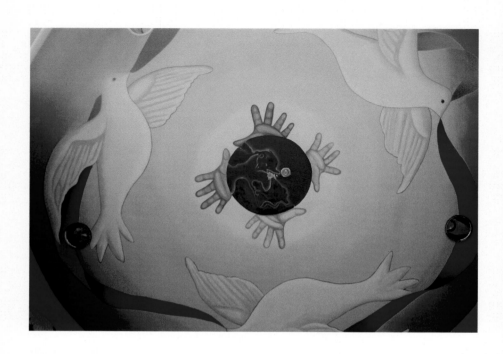

Sammy has the final word.

The Challenge: Fullness of Life for All.

PART VI

Saved by Love

—❯—

Nothing we do, however virtuous, could be accomplished alone; therefore, we must be saved by love. No virtuous act is quite as virtuous from the standpoint of our friend or foe as it is from our own standpoint; therefore, we must be saved by the final form of love, which is forgiveness.

REINHOLD NIEBUHR,
THE IRONY OF AMERICAN HISTORY

CHAPTER 25

Spiritual Warfare

We cannot deny the spiritual battle that is raging around us. There is good and there is evil. Evil is very strong. We cannot look the other way. Our children will not survive in this world today unless we pray, walk, work, move, march, teach, and—yes!—sing, on and on and on, for peace and hope and goodness.

My alarm wakes me early on this cloudy Thursday morning. It is May 19, 2005, the day of the Community of Peace Academy Tenth Anniversary Annual Meeting and Spring Program, and there is much to do. Last weekend I was totally consumed in writing two federal grants that were due on Monday, and I've been behind ever since. This morning I will think through the business of the annual meeting and prepare some brief remarks. The weekly faculty bulletin is due today as well, and there will be no time for such things once the busyness of the school day sweeps me away.

I finish my work and arrive at school unusually late, but still in time to give the morning announcements: "Good morning everyone! Today is Thursday, May 19, and it is specialists' day one. Happy birthday to Ms. Vaughn and Mr. Zbacnik! If you should see them today, be sure to wish them a very happy birthday! At 9:30 this morning, Ms. Molden's class will be picking up the recycling bins. Thank you, boys and girls! We really appreciate your good work."

The big news today is the annual meeting and spring program. I continue: "There will be rehearsals in the gym throughout the day today. Gym classes will be held in classrooms. Students, we hope that all of you will come to the spring program this evening and bring your parents with you. This is a reminder that everyone must go home on the buses this afternoon as usual. The doors will open this evening at 6:15." Following the announcements, I give the lunch and breakfast menus and then, after wishing everyone a pleasant day, invite them to stand for the Pledge of Allegiance and the PeaceBuilder's Pledge. All is well.

Next I check my mail box. Among the papers, I find a small red box tied with a ribbon. This surprise package is from Jen Drier, one of our special education teachers. She has been with us since September. The note reads, "Happy Tenth Spring Meeting/Concert! When I saw this, I thought of you, so decided you should have it. I wish I could express my gratitude to you for providing such a safe shelter for kindness and support. I absolutely LOVE THIS SCHOOL and my new family at CPA (and that's saying a lot since you've seen how many schools I've been at)." Inside the box is a pewter peace dove inscribed with the words, "There is no way to peace. Peace is the way. a. j. muste." This unexpected gift touches my heart and I search my office for the perfect spot for it. After hanging it on the wall near my desk, I check phone messages.

There are three: one from a charter school director in Wisconsin asking to schedule a visit the following Wednesday, one from a professor asking for an interview regarding his dissertation, and one from Aaron Benner. Aaron says he is forwarding a message from one of our frequent guest teachers. He has just accepted a full-time job and will no longer be subbing at our school. I listen with pleasure:

"Aaron, this is Tom Finnegan calling. I wanted to express my gratitude for the opportunity to work with you and your students. They are really terrific kids. Their opportunity should be enormous. Continue to do the great job you are doing with them. I'm going to miss them more than any group. They are dear and wonderful kids. Give them my regrets and my regards and my hopes for their success. Tell them to continue working hard and being good kids. You have a great school and a great set-up. It's the best place I've ever worked."

E-mail is next. I send out a message inviting the staff to send me their special thoughts regarding our Lunch Ladies who will be receiving the Community Member of the Year Award from the board of directors at the annual meeting this evening. I plan to incorporate staff comments into my remarks. These four women are much loved by all. They were chosen by unanimous decision to receive this award, which is given to those who show an exceptional generosity of spirit.

I have thirteen messages and no time. I scroll through them quickly as Greg Buckner appears at my door. We have a 9:30 meeting to discuss replacing the old slate boards with white boards in the 1938 section of the building. Having received the teachers' input regarding preferred locations for white boards and bulletin boards, we are trying to find continuity. We make some progress, and Greg leaves with a plan.

I am reviewing the agenda for the evening when Bonnie, our office manager, pops in and advises me to look out my window. My office is just to the right of our main entrance. I am surprised to find the corner of Magnolia and Burr engulfed by two large fire trucks and an array of police and rescue vehicles. They arrived silently and now, firemen and policemen are everywhere. The center of this unexpected activity is the gray house on the corner. This house is kitty-corner from my parking spot. Bonnie suggests that I might want to find out what is going on. She takes good care of me.

It is a gray, chilly morning. I grab my coat and my keys and head for the parking lot doors. As I approach the scene, I am trying to grasp what might be happening. Men is white suits and wearing gas masks add an eerie, surreal effect. I feel off balance. I see a policeman standing on the boulevard, just a few yards from my car, and I approach him. I introduce myself as the principal of the school and ask what is happening. He tells me that this a Ramsey County operation and that he is here representing the city. He tells me that they think there is a meth lab in the house. I ask what we need to do. He tells me that we should keep the children inside the building until we are given an all-clear. He takes my name and phone number and tells me that as soon as the Ramsey County official arrives, he will tell him to call me.

I return to the building and give my report to Bonnie and the office staff. Bonnie makes an all school announcement that students and staff are to stay inside the building until further notice. It is 10:57. I send an all staff alert via e-mail:

Dear Staff,

At the present time, Ramsey County is in the process of searching the house on the corner of Magnolia and Burr for a possible meth lab. We have been advised that this could take a few hours. We have been advised to keep the students in the building until further notice.

We will keep you posted. Please do not discuss this with students.

Thank you,
Dr. Rusthoven

A sense of uncertainty and numbness ensues. Yellow tape locks us in at both ends of the street. We are under siege. Bonnie soon returns with her assistant. She is obviously distressed. She says, to no one in particular, that this is very serious. Meth labs are terribly toxic and can explode. Our kindergartens are at that end of the building. Maybe we should be moving the children.

I assure her that I am certain that the authorities would not allow us to be exposed to danger, but to set everyone's minds at ease, I will go and ask more questions. Once again, I grab my coat and keys and head for the door. As I scan the scene, one of the masked men is carrying a container out of the house. He carries it with great care. A person wrapped in a white sheet is escorted into a waiting police car.

This time, I walk bravely into the street. A fireman approaches me. Again I introduce myself. I explain the concerns that have been raised, and he quickly assures me that we are not in danger. The fire trucks have been strategically positioned so as to protect the school. The wind is blowing away from the building, and all of the dangerous chemicals have been removed. With sadness in his eyes and heaviness in his voice, he informs me that they have found the worst living conditions they have ever seen. He tells me that the couple who ran the lab are both in their thirties, but looked like old people. Tragically, they have carried a nine-month-old baby out of the lower level. Our precious grandchild is thirteen months old. I am beyond grief.

Like a character in a bad movie, I return to the building. Immediately, I send out an Alert Update. It is 11:29:

Dear Staff,

This is to assure you that there is no threat to our safety resulting from the investigation on the corner of Magnolia and Burr. Please keep students inside the building until an all-clear is given.

Thank you,
Dr. Rusthoven

Shortly after, the Ramsey County officer calls. He is outside, and I tell him I'll come out. He is a pleasant young man with a heavy heart. He repeats what the fireman told me and adds that two school-aged children also lived in the house. My mind is trying to comprehend their reality; how they awoke this morning amidst the fumes and squalor and somehow got themselves together and left for school. Did anyone, anywhere know? Were there any signs that these children lived a nightmare? If they attended our school, would we have known? These questions haunt me. The officer and I exchange our painful thoughts regarding this immediate tragedy. He is on his way to the school to take the children into protective custody.

When I return to my office, my e-mail is a welcome distraction. Messages for the Lunch Ladies are arriving in abundance and they lift my spirits.

> I am always amazed at the level of familiarity they have with our students. They know most of the students' names and are able to talk with them on a very personal level. I also appreciate the generosity they share with me in use of space. I'm sure most of the staff feels as comfortable and welcomed in the kitchen and the lunch area. That is no small feat, it would be easier for them to isolate themselves in their work but I feel they work hard at being a central part of our community both as individuals and as a comfortable place. Great Selection! I whole heartily agree!

> I have worked in many schools and have known many "lunch ladies" . . . NEVER before have I had the privilege of working with such kind, caring, flexible and fun lunch people. I'm a 38 year old who can't seem to come down for lunch at a lunch time (it's usually transition times) and who CAN'T remember her own lunch number. In any of the other schools, I would have been ignored or belittled but at CPA Nancy, Ruthy, Amanda, and Latrice go out of their way to help me AND make sure that I leave with a smile. I feel special when I see them.

> My work here is enjoyable due to the pleasant greetings I receive from Nancy, Ruthy, Amanda and Latrice. I feel they live out the mission of Community of Peace Academy to value every person. I feel blessed to work with them!

At 12:35, I realize that I am hungry. This is my day to supervise the high school lunch. It starts at 1:10, so I head for the faculty room and a needed break. The faculty room is at the corner of Magnolia and Burr. The drama unfolds directly outside the windows. Mr. Xiong is standing at the window looking out. Our minds, if not our eyes, are on this extraordinary turn of events. We cannot escape it.

We visit as we eat together. There is concern about the evening program. Will they really finish the cleanup on time. What will happen at dismissal? The buses use the street that is blocked off. How could parents do this to their children? How could we not have known?

I am in the middle of my sandwich when Bonnie comes in to tell me that there are reporters in the office from Channel 11 and Channel 5. They want to interview me. I leave my lunch as is and head for the office. I introduce myself and invite them into my office. When the three of us are seated, I begin calmly. I ask what they have in mind. I need reassurance that they will not try to sensationalize the position of the school. The story is not about us. This needs to be about the children who were living in the house. I assure them that the authorities have handled the situation with great care on our behalf. Their responses put my mind at ease, and I agree to be interviewed. I ask them to wait for me in the outer office. I need a moment to gather my thoughts. I call Tim McGowan to tell him I'll be late getting to the cafeteria for the high school lunch. Outside my window, I can see the TV crews setting up their cameras. I grab my coat and head for the front door.

The seriousness of the moment grips me. Another reporter has joined us. I have not met her, and she is obviously out for a good story. Three small boxes, are attached to my jacket, and a microphone is fastened to my lapel. They ask me to zip my coat to hide the wires, and we are ready.

I field their questions thoughtfully. I thank Ramsey County and the St. Paul authorities for their good work and for the care they used in ensuring the safety of the school. The new reporter asks how I feel about having a meth lab so close to the school? She talks about the dangers and asks if I fear that there may be other meth labs close by. I state that the danger, the tragedy, is the children who live in such houses and that there are such houses in every community. This is a very serious social issue and one that all of us should be concerned about. She keeps pressuring for more, until I finally state that the interview is over.

Numbly, I return to my office and take off my coat. While my son, Benjamin, was in treatment the previous January, he informed us that meth was his drug of choice. As recently as two weeks before, he told me that he still thinks about it every day and he still has a pipe. I feel a sudden need to talk to him, to plead with him never, ever to use it again. Impulsively, I rush to the phone and start dialing his number. Then, I catch myself and hang up. I am too emotional to be rational. My timing might be bad. I need time to think. Within moments, the phone rings and it is Ben. I am stunned.

I tell him that I am in the midst of a crisis and I explain the day's events. I tell him that I wanted to call him and had decided against it, but that since he called me, it must be divine providence. I tell him that I know he is a grown man and I have no right to tell him what to do, but I plead with him to throw the pipe away and to remain strong. I tell him that using meth is like injecting the HIV virus directly into your veins. It will kill you, just as surely and painfully. I tell him that the forces of evil are alive and well and that this is the work of evil. I tell him what a wonderful, beautiful person he is and that God has a purpose for his life. He tells me that he knows these things. That his friends tell him how much they like him the way he is now and that he is different when he uses.

I remind him that he is baptized and that he belongs to God, not Satan. He listens quietly. He tells me that he likes to hear me say these things. He says that he does belong to God. He assures me that he is doing well and that God is helping him. He says that every time he thinks about meth, something intervenes. He calls it divine intervention. He says that he has a good support group. He tells me that he will stop by the house on Saturday morning. I tell him to bring the pipe. He says, "I love you," and I hang up. Almost without thought, I head for the cafeteria. I am off balance.

As I enter the cafeteria, Molly Heisenfelt, the school social worker, approaches me. She asks if I am all right. I hadn't thought about how I might look at this moment. I take a deep breath and try to regain my composure. I fill her in on the interview. She gives me a hug. Tim McGowan joins us and makes a joke about the interviews to lighten our spirits. He, too, is concerned for me.

Some students come over and make small talk. They need reassurance as well. Tim says he will stay in the cafeteria and encourages me to go and finish my lunch. I realize how much I need a break and I go gratefully. One of the teachers has carefully packed up my lunch for me and has left me a caring note. I think about how grateful I am for the good people who work with me.

When I return to my office, I have word from Lou Trudeau that we will need to dismiss from the other side of the building today. The police have notified our transportation providers and they will send extra support at dismissal to assist us. I send out another e-mail:

1:23 p.m.

Dear Staff,

The Ramsey County authorities did find a large meth lab in the house across the street from the school. We will be dismissing today from the DeSoto side of the building. We are told that they will be finished with the cleanup process in time to proceed with our program tonight. We will be sending a notice home with students.

You may tell students that the people in the house were making illegal drugs. This is a very serious offense, especially since they lived so near our school. Please assure students that they were not in danger and that the people will not be back. We needed to stay out of the way today so the firemen and police could do their work.

This will be on the news tonight. There were two school aged children and a 9 month old baby living with their parents in the house. Pray for them. Thank you to all of you.

Dr. Rusthoven

Amidst my deep thoughts, I hear the sound of youthful voices singing. It is a song that I love and I am drawn to it, like a desert traveler to a clear, cool stream. As I enter the gym, I am greeted by the words, "No storm can shake my inmost calm, while to that rock I'm clinging; Since love is lord of heav'n and earth, how can I keep from singing?" It is the Choraliers, our middle school choir, and their music sweeps over my soul and makes me strong. Throughout the afternoon beautiful music wafts from the gym and washes over us, keeping us calm and serene as the work goes on outside our windows. Had our lockdown happened on another day, it would surely have been more difficult to bear.

At 2:17, I decide to send out a positive e-mail to raise our thoughts beyond this moment:

Dear Staff,

PeaceBuilders is considering Community of Peace as a possible "Show Case" site for their program. A gentleman will be visiting us on Monday, May 23 at 10:00 a.m.

If our school is chosen, we would receive updated materials and training free of charge. We could also expect to be visited by people who want to see PeaceBuilders in action.

Sincerely,
Dr. Rusthoven

At 2:23, I receive Lou's e-mail regarding the notice that would be sent to parents:

Dear Parent/Mentor

Today Ramsey County authorities and the St. Paul police and fire departments cleaned out a meth lab that was operating in a house across Magnolia Street and across Burr Street from the school.

Both city and county authorities took great care to assure the safety of our students and staff.

Due to this emergency, we did not have outside recess today and dismissal took place on DeSoto Street, a block away from the house. There was news coverage of this event, so you may see it reported on television.

Sincerely,
Louis Trudeau
Elementary Assistant Principal

As the afternoon wears on, it occurs to me that there are people I need to call. Ken Pugh, our board chair, should hear the news from me. I call, but he is not in, so I leave the message with his wife. She expresses her care and offers words of encouragement. I tell her to ask Ken to come to the annual meeting early so that we can talk. Since I will be on the news tonight, I need to inform my dad so he won't be alarmed. As I am making this call, Choua Pa comes to my door. She is in the tenth grade and she is married and pregnant. She wants to talk to me about the tenth-grade trip. I ask her to wait across the hall, and, after I reach Dad, I invite her to come in. She is a sweet child, and she is obviously troubled.

She tells me that she really wants to go on the class trip to the International Wolf Center in Ely, but her mother won't sign the papers. She is also worried because now the trip is next week and she doesn't have the thirty dollars to pay for the trip. I tell her not to worry about the money, that no one misses trips for lack of money. I need to know why her mother won't sign the papers. She tells me that her mother is a Hmong shaman. The traditional Hmong religion is animism. Choua Pa says that her mother has told her that if you go into the woods or near water when you are pregnant, evil spirits will come into you and they will harm the baby. She says that she is now married in the Hmong way, so she is living with her husband's family. They are Christian and she wants to be Christian too. She says that her mother-in-law says that if you believe in evil spirits, then it is true, but if you don't believe in it, it is not true. Choua Pa doesn't believe in it, so she thinks she could go and it wouldn't hurt the baby. She wants to know what I think.

I ask who is responsible for her. Is her husband's family responsible for her, or is her mother responsible for her? At this point, I ask Choua Pa if it would be all right to invite Mr. Xiong to join us. She nods her approval. I find Mr. Xiong at his computer. I explain the situation and invite him to come to my office. We pick up where we left off. Mr. Xiong says that in Hmong tradition, Choua Pa has now become the responsibility of her in-laws. In America, however, her parents are still legally responsible because of her age. I ask Mr. Xiong if he would call Choua Pa's mother. I suggest that he tell her that this is a study trip for science; that there are classrooms at the Wolf Center and Choua Pa will not need to be out in the woods or near water. He assures us that he will call and that he is quite sure that her mother will give her permission.

Choua Pa then looks at us earnestly and says, "My husband's family is Catholic. I want to be Catholic, but I am not baptized yet. Do you think it would be all right if I were to be a little bit afraid? Sometimes, I get a little bit afraid. Do you think then evil spirits could come into me?"

Mr. Xiong answers in his calm fatherly way. "I am a hunter. Sometimes when I hunt, it gets dark and I have to walk back to my car through the woods. If I imagine that something is coming, I am afraid and I walk fast. If I think it is running after me, then I run." He laughs his jolly laugh. "This is all in my head! We make ourselves afraid by our thinking."

I enter the conversation cautiously. "Choua Pa, no one can tell us what to believe. We must decide for ourselves. For me, I have decided to be a Christian. In the Bible, the words that Jesus said more than any other words were, 'Fear not.' I am a Christian because I have chosen to not be afraid. Instead, I believe that God loves us and watches over us. This makes me happy. That's why I smile all the time." Everyone has to choose what they believe.

Choua Pa is listening intently. She says, "Some people say they see ghosts. Is that because they believe in ghosts?" Mr. Xiong says he thinks that is true. He affirms again that if we don't believe in spirits, they will not trouble us. Choua Pa turns her thoughts back to the thirty dollars. She is restating all the reasons she doesn't have the money. I take her face in my hands and say gently, "Fear not." She smiles. We assure her that Mr. Xiong will call her mother. She thanks us, and I give her a hug before she leaves.

At dismissal, the sun is shining. Everyone is present to assist, and the process goes more smoothly than we had hoped or imagined. Yellow tape, media vans, and emergency vehicles remain in force just around the corner and out of sight. At 4:13, Lou sends an All Staff e-mail:

Great teamwork at today's dismissal!!
Thank you for all your help.
Comment from a Transportation Official who was on the
scene . . . "It was a piece of cake".

Lou

The building empties quickly after dismissal. The staff will be returning at 6:15 and everyone needs a break. My husband arrives just before five, and we leave for a quick supper at our favorite neighborhood restaurant. Lou joins us. As we eat, we watch the TV monitor for the local news, but see no report of the event that is still unfolding outside our school.

When we return to the building, there is another news van parked in the parking lot just behind my parking spot. The yellow tape has been removed, and most of the emergency vehicles are gone. I send staff members out to greet parents and students as they arrive and I stand at the door greeting people as they enter. A seventh-grade student, who I have been told is a friend of the children who lived in the house, stops to tell me that she saw me on the news. She tells me quietly and earnestly that she liked what I said. Her remark soothes my troubled spirit.

When I finally enter the building, Ken is there. I invite him into my office and he hands me a caring note from his wife. I thank him and am truly touched by her kindness. We review the agenda for the annual meeting and program. I will facilitate, but Ken will conduct most of the business: board recognition and elections, Community Member of the Year Award, Five and Ten Year Service Awards. It will be an eventful evening.

Our program is well attended, and the challenges of the day give way to joy as we are surrounded by beautiful music and expressions of love and appreciation. The walls of the gym are decorated with colorful artwork. Members leaving the board are applauded and new members voted in. The lunch ladies are radiant in their spring colors. Wearing rose corsages and bright smiles, they graciously receive the cheers and loving words of thanks that are heaped upon them. Staff members who have been with the school for five and ten years are called forward to receive their awards. This is a new tradition, so nearly thirty receive five-year awards. Eight of us have been with the school since the first year. In spite of a request to hold applause, students cheer and yell as each teacher or staff member comes forward. Finally, we fill the risers as we stand to accept the warm congratulations of all.

Amidst the business of the evening, the children bless us with their amazing music. Song after song brings messages of hope, peace, and love. The Academy Choir amazes me still again, with their powerful arrangement of "Bridge over Troubled Water." When the staff choir comes forward, it is evident that we are charged to sing our song. The message is powerful and our day has given us renewed resolve in delivering it. Written by Ysaye M. Barnwell and entitled, "Hope," the song is sung a cappella, accompanied only by the beat of a hand drum. It begins in unison and gradually builds to five parts, a powerful, moving chant.

> *If we want hope to survive in this world today,*
> *then every day we've got to pray on, pray on!*
> *If we want hope to survive in this world today,*
> *then every day, we've got to pray on.*

Then the tenors take it. They sing with resolved strength:

> *If we want hope to survive in this world today,*
> *then every day we've got to walk on, walk on!*
> *If we want hope to survive in this world today,*
> *then every day we've got to walk on.*

Joined by the second tenors:

> *We've got to walk on, walk on!*
> *We've got to walk on, walk on!*
> *We've got to walk on, walk on!*
> *We've got to walk on, walk on!*

Next the altos:

If we want peace in the world,
we've got to work on, work on, work on!
If we want peace in the world,
we've got to work on, work on, work on!

Add the basses:

We've got to move on!
We've got to move on!
We've got to move on!
We've got to move on!

Then above it all the sopranos enter:

March on!
March on!
March on!
March on!

Next all voices softly:

If we want peace in the world,
we've got to teach on, teach on, teach on!
If we want peace in the world,
we've got to teach on, teach on, teach on!

On to the rousing climax:

If we want hope to survive in this world today,
then every day we've got to sing on, sing on!
If we want peace in the world,
we've got to sing on, sing on, sing on! Sing On!

Next the Academy Choir, with its signature number, "You've Got a Friend."

> *Over any mountain, no matter when,*
> *through the darkest valley again and again,*
> *I'll be there beside you beginning to end.*
> *You've got a friend. You've got a friend!*

Their voices fill the room as everyone claps to the beat.

The staff choir enthusiastically returns to the risers for our finale, "We Rise Again!" Brian Conners and I lead off with these words:

> *When the waves roll on over the waters, and the ocean cries;*
> *We look to our sons and daughters to explain our lives.*
> *As if a child could tell us why, that as sure as the sunrise,*
> *as sure as the sea,*
> *as sure as the wind in the trees;*

And then, the choirs, eighty strong, join in on this remarkable refrain:

> *We rise again in the faces of our children.*
> *We rise again in the voices of their songs.*
> *We rise again in the waves out on the ocean,*
> *and then . . . we rise again!*

As the song builds toward its extraordinary climax, the power of the moment touches us all. We feel safe and protected and blessed.

When my husband and I return to my office, Tim McGowan comes to tell me that during the program, he found the parents of one of our students attempting to rob the kitchen. He had noticed them leaving and followed them. They were totally caught off guard by his presence and made excuses that made no sense. He gently shepherded them upstairs and did not accuse them. They are ensnared by drugs, as are so many. We must always be vigilant and on guard for the sake of the children. I thank Tim for his good work, and we say goodnight. Before leaving, I send out the Faculty Facts for the coming week. We will go on.

That night we watch the news. I am appalled by pictures of the interior of the house that hid such misery from my view for so long. I moan at the sight of the fireman carrying the baby out, its tiny eyes straining against the unfamiliar light of day. The mother and infant were found on the lowest level of the house, and we are told that meth fumes move downward, making the lowest level the most toxic.

I go to bed, but I can't sleep. I get up at midnight and read a devotional book to change my thinking. When I awaken, I go to my office and look for a poem. I find it unfinished, scratched on an old envelope. Ironically, I began writing it two weeks earlier. It is titled "Dark Houses," and as I reread my writing, I am stunned by its relevance. It seems as though I had a premonition. I go to my computer and finish the poem.

> *Dark houses.*
> *Where shades*
> *block out the light of day*
> *and beds*
> *have no legs.*
> *Where fathers*
> *do their work at midnight*
> *and mothers sleep all day*
> *While policemen watch.*
>
> *Dark houses.*
> *Where stoical children*
> *tend crying babies*
> *and no one tells.*

Where dreams die young
and nightmares last all day
While hunger and fear
turn hope to despair.

Dark houses.
Where death is made
and sold for the price of a soul.
Where parents
buy a one way ticket to hell
and take the family with them
While Satan laughs.

Poetry helps me clear my head. Having expressed these thoughts, I feel a sense of relief. Mr. Xiong is right, we must control our minds or our negative thoughts and fears take over. I set the poem aside and prepare for another day.

I check my e-mail and find a message from Tim Danz:

Karen,

We've learned that two of the girls in the house across the street from the school have friends here at CPA. Some of our girls know them and have great concern for them. I'm wondering if there is any way for our students to get cards or letters to them. Do you have any information or know who we might contact?

Tim D

Friday begins with a half day of computer training. There are bugs in the system, and I find it hard to concentrate. I have a meeting at one o'clock to discuss our options for bringing a school-based clinic to Community of Peace Academy. Results of the Minnesota Student Survey and our concerns regarding student pregnancies have caused us to explore this possibility. Space is an issue—we don't have enough of it. The meeting involves the Ramsey County Family Life educator who has worked at our school for seven years, our school nurse, and our architect. The meeting is still going on at 2:30, and I excuse myself. The staff is giving an unusual baby shower after school, and I must prepare the faculty room.

This year, two or our families have lost their mothers. Our shower is for a baby boy whose mother died in childbirth two months ago. The baby's two brothers and one sister are our students. We are giving the shower, with the father's permission, to show our love and care for the family.

Shortly after I reach the faculty room, others arrive to help me. Soon the room is arranged with flowers on the tables, a table filled with beautifully wrapped gifts, and a table laden with a cake decorated in yellow and blue and a bowl of punch. The children arrive first and then the teachers and members of the staff. The father arrives last with the baby. He is a lovely child, dressed in yellow and sleeping peacefully. They have named him Tou Ger, meaning last son. His father hands him to me.

Mr. Xiong is here, as well as several other Hmong staff members, to make sure that the family will feel comfortable. Mr. Xiong asks if I would like to say something. I give words of welcome and express our care and support. Mr. Xiong interprets my words, and the father begins to cry. He tells us that it is hard without his wife and thanks us for helping his family.

Tim Danz and Nico Zbacnik are present. They both teach the oldest son, who is in the eighth grade. Tim is a caring, compassionate father of two boys. He holds the baby and rocks him as the children open the presents. Kay Buzza and Terri Kramar also take turns rocking this precious child. Kay teaches first grade and has an infant grandchild. Terri is a young mother who also teaches first grade. We do not speak our thoughts of the infant across the street. We do what we can.

When the shower has ended, I find that the decision regarding the health clinic remains unresolved. The only possible option will require that my office is remodeled. I will lose two windows in the process. I will have two left. I can live with two. If others can agree on this plan, I will sign off on it. We part, somewhat hopeful.

On Saturday morning, Ben arrives at the house as planned. He greets me with a hug and tells me that he saw me on TV. We go to the kitchen and I ask him to come and sit down. I have something I want to share with him. He pulls out a glass object and sets it on the table. "Here it is." He tells me that it is a meth pipe and he explains how it works. I hand him a copy of my poem and ask him to read it. When he finishes, he says, "Come with me." I follow him to the back door. He continues, "I don't even want you to think the things you are thinking." I ask where he is going and he tells me that he is going to throw the pipe down the sewer. I watch him walk to the corner. He throws it down the sewer and walks back to the house. We never mention it again.

I am left to ponder all these things. We cannot deny the spiritual battle that is raging around us. There is good and there is evil. Evil is very strong. We cannot look the other way. Our children will not survive in this world today unless we pray, walk, work, move, march, teach, and—yes!—sing, on and on and on, for peace and hope and goodness. We do rise again in the faces of our children. They are the hope of our future. We must courageously tap into all the forces of goodness at our disposal in order to save them.

CHAPTER 26

Love in Action

The best way to ensure that no child will be left behind is to ensure that those responsible for the education of all children are people who love them. Quality education, like good parenting, requires a long-term commitment. It requires good stewardship, and it requires sacrifice. Those who have the power to do so would be wise to return public education to parents and teachers.

When I was in college, I spent my summers counseling at a camp in northern Minnesota. I was responsible for planning and directing the daily activities of my small group of campers. Archery was one of the activities, and it was not my forte. One day, however, as I was demonstrating the proper use of the equipment, stance, and technique, I pulled back the bow and to my surprise, I hit a bulls-eye! In my astonishment, I remained cool and collected and soaked in the girls' admiration. I have never forgotten the incident.

As executive director of a charter school, it is my responsibility to keep the board of directors well informed of all of the business of the school. Each month, I prepare a packet of information that is sent to the board on the Friday prior to the meeting. Preparing these packets is an intense process. A school is a dynamic environment, and information of interest to the board comes in almost daily. I often find myself stopping the copier to add just one more item to the packet.

School boards in large urban districts oversee the work of

countless schools. In St. Paul, which is considered to be a small city, the school board is responsible for the oversight of programs and schools that fill nearly two full pages in the phone book. Decisions made by such boards must of necessity be general in nature, yet the needs of individual students within individual schools are often quite specific.

Within large districts, politics play a large role in the operation of school boards. Budget constraints often mandate decisions that have far-reaching results. Even when intended for good, the decisions of such boards often miss the mark. At worst, they often impact particular schools and students negatively. As my brief encounter with archery taught me, if we hope to hit the bull's-eye, we must be within reasonable distance of the target. The chance of hitting the bull's-eye becomes more remote as the target is moved farther and farther away.

My first experience with school boards was as principal of a small Catholic grade school in south Minneapolis. The members of this board all belonged to the same parish. Most were parents of the children who attended the school. They knew one another and they knew one another's children. They attended church together, served church dinners together, and went on camping trips together. The decisions made by this board were never general. They were always specific. They were made for the benefit of their own beloved children. They seldom missed the mark.

Lack of funds was a constant challenge. There was never enough money to give the children all they deserved. Stewardship becomes essential under such circumstances. People learn to be good stewards of the things they have. Sacrifice is essential. People will and do sacrifice out of love. Parents worked long hours at fundraising activities. They sold candy and spring bedding plants. They held rummage sales and pancake breakfasts. They took over the concession stands at the Metrodome for Twins games and Vikings games. All that they earned provided programs and equipment for their children. In addition to raising funds, these many activities strengthened relationships within the community that surrounded the children and their school.

When Community of Peace Academy opened in September of 1995, the school did not have access to federal Title I funds, nor did it have access to any state or federal start-up grants. We were, as the saying goes, "operating on a shoestring." Teachers were all paid the same: $23,000. As principal, I was paid $31,000. Apart from salaries, we had exactly $43,000 to provide a program for 160 students. Having previously been a Catholic school administrator, this was familiar territory.

We were able to lease space in a Catholic school building that, due to a consolidation, was nearly abandoned. Teachers, parents, students, and friends gathered on a hot, late-summer day and began washing windows, cleaning classrooms, and cleaning and moving furniture. We found sources of free used office furniture and school desks. Despite the heat and humidity, my husband and his friends transported and unloaded these items (more than once), carrying them up flights of stairs to various classrooms. We bought plastic chairs for the kindergarten at K-Mart and dictionaries at Target. These stories were fondly retold at the celebration of our tenth anniversary.

Since nearly 90 percent of our students qualified for free and reduced-price meals, our Title I funding arrived midyear. As a former Catholic school principal, I was astounded by the amount. This new money enabled us to extend our kindergarten program from all day every other day, to an every day program. Money was earmarked for library books. Over 70 percent of our students were recent Hmong immigrants for whom English was their second language. Title I funds made it possible to contract with the ESL department at Hamline University to provide ESL classes for all of our teachers. When I was informed by the state Title I coordinator late that first year that our school qualified for an addition $50,000 in federal funding, I asked incredulously, "What will we do with all that money?" She never let me forget it.

In 2004, education/evolving, a joint venture of the Center for Policy Studies and Hamline University, did a study titled "More Money or Different Spending Choices?" The study looked at spending patterns of 338 districts and sixty charter schools in Minnesota to identify which ten of each category spent the largest percentage of their expenditures on instruction, regardless of whether overall spending was high or low. Striking similarities were found among the identified districts and charter schools.

All of the ten districts that spent the largest portion of their budget on instruction were small rural districts. For charter schools, those operated by teacher cooperatives (in which a collection of teachers is the decision maker) were disproportionately represented in the top ten. The study reported that those districts and schools tightly managed their budgets, with an overarching spending principle that students came first—the needs of their students drove spending choices. They seemed to share a decision-making structure that was transparent and especially close to teachers, students, and parents. Community of Peace Academy was among the top ten charter schools identified.

This study raises some interesting questions about stewardship, sacrifice, and the financing of public education. Having administered an urban, high-poverty school for more than ten years, I can attest to the fact that the needs are many. I can also attest to the fact that financial resources are available to meet the needs. Community of Peace Academy operates under the principle of *unconditional positive regard for all*. This is a "love" principle. When a school operates in this way and those closest to the children are given full authority to make decisions about how resources will be allocated, most of the money, most of the time, will be used to benefit the children. Given this truth, it is not surprising that all ten of the traditional school districts so identified were small rural districts.

On October 13, 2004, the Minnesota Department of Education and the Teaching Commission held a luncheon for Minnesota leaders titled "A Call to Action on Teacher Quality." Among the invited guests and members were W. James McNerney, chairman of 3M; Minnesota Business Partnership; the Minnesota High Tech Association; MnSCU, P-16 Council; and the Minnesota Chamber of Commerce. The luncheon speaker was Louis V. Gerstner Jr., former chairman of IBM Corporation, and founder and chair of the Teaching Commission. The purpose of this auspicious event was to share the report published by the Teaching Commission and to introduce Governor Tim Pawlenty's initiative on teacher quality.

The governor announced that Minnesota was the first state that would implement the recommendations of the Teaching Commission. Those in attendance were informed that in the current transition from an industrial age to an information age, the United States was falling behind and that one thing that would make the difference in putting the U.S. ahead internationally was putting a highly qualified teacher in every classroom. Among the recommendations of the commission are increasing teachers' pay, pay for performance, and paying teachers more who go into urban schools. We were told that the governor would put more money into K–12 education to support these initiatives.

Minnesota's Call to Action on Teacher Quality is an "I–It" initiative. It mirrors nearly every current public school initiative in America. It assumes that teachers are widgets that can be manipulated by money and that children are widgets that, if properly manipulated, will put the United States ahead in the international race. Teachers deserve to be paid justly. However, it is not money that inspires good teaching. The assumption that money will entice good teachers to venture into urban communities is flawed. Teachers who teach in urban schools must feel an affinity for the families and children who live there. They must see them as the "Thou" and not as an "It." This is the first requirement of good teaching. It is a "quality" that money cannot buy.

At the close of his remarks, the governor read from an article written by a teacher in which she remarked that someone had asked her what she makes, to which she answered, "I make a difference.

What do you make?" The teacher went on to eloquently describe the real work of teaching. Having read her remarks, the governor stated, "I appreciate that kind of commitment, but it is not enough."

That kind of commitment may not be enough, but it is absolutely essential. In large urban areas all across America, Catholic schools have, for decades, been islands of hope providing quality education in the shadow of dysfunctional public schools. The driving force behind the success of these schools is love. If our corporate leaders care about the future of our country, they would be well advised to take note of this. Quality teaching requires qualities of character that are not for sale at any price.

Jawanza Kunjufu (1986), African American writer and lecturer, opens all of his teacher workshops by declaring, "You cannot teach a child who you do not love. You cannot teach a child who you do not respect. You cannot teach a child who you do not understand. You cannot teach a child who you are afraid of. You cannot teach a child without bonding first, which results from love, respect, and understanding." If we hope to close the gap, our first requirement of every teacher, must be to love, respect, and understand the children and youth they teach; to want the same for their students as they would want for their own dear children.

Love inspires love. Teachers who feel loved and respected within their school communities are empowered and inspired to love in return. Love, I–Thou relationships, unconditional positive regard for all—these qualities, not money, are what drive high-quality education.

The U.S. Department of Education (2004) has published a National Education Technology Plan called *Toward a New Golden Age in American Education*. The initiatives set forth in this plan are admirable and essential to our future. However, there will be no "golden age" in American education until we return the education of public school children to those who love them best.

The information age has made our world a very small place.

Distance no longer separates us from our neighbors on the other side of the globe. We are instantly made aware of happenings everywhere and can communicate verbal and visual messages to anyone, anywhere, in an instant. These recent developments have great potential for international good and perhaps even greater potential for international evil. The moral character of our citizens will determine, more than any other factor, America's future and our place in the international community.

If the public education establishment continues to wander in a spiritual wilderness, where I–It relationships prevail, hundreds of thousands of our nation's children will not find wholeness and fullness of life, nor will they gain the moral strength to make decisions and choices that will ensure the goodwill of others. This is the greatest threat to the future of our nation and world.

Educating our nation's children is hard work. There are no easy answers to the challenges that public education faces. There are no quick fixes that will ensure that we leave no child behind. The work before us will not be accomplished in four years, or eight years, or during anyone's term of office. It will require a lifelong commitment to giving the very best we have to offer.

The best way to ensure that no child will be left behind is to ensure that those responsible for the education of all children are people who love them. Quality education, like good parenting, requires a long-term commitment. It requires good stewardship, and it requires sacrifice. Those who have the power to do so would be wise to return public education to parents and teachers.

The frequent argument that, if given the chance to choose, parents of poor children will not make good choices regarding their children's schools, is a weak argument. In my experience, only those parents who are mentally ill or severely addicted may seem, during their bad episodes, not to care for their children. The vast majority of parents love their children, want them to be loved by others, and would choose a school with a loving environment and loving faculty in a heartbeat, if given the opportunity to do so.

When given the ability to choose their assignments, and when given autonomy over their work, teachers become the best judges of what will benefit their teaching and their students. Teachers who feel an affinity for the parents of their students, who stand in solidarity with them and are committed to working with them, will be more successful in educating their students. Teachers who love their students and who feel loved and empowered to do their work are the most powerful force for educational reform in America.

Educating the children of our country is sacred work. It requires patience, courage, sacrifice, humility, forgiveness, and love. Public schools that commit themselves to this vision have potential to transform the lives of their students and all members of their school community; to empower and inspire them to freely choose wholeness and fullness of life *for all*. The power in this precept would transform our nation and our world, one public school graduate at a time.

CHAPTER 27

The Final Form of Love

If our nation's public schools are to be transformed in our lifetime, they will be transformed by the highest form of love, which is forgiveness. This new vision transcends our political, social, racial, cultural, and religious differences. We must reach across all such barriers for the sake of our children. Our work will be immeasurably enriched, and our own lives will be transformed in the process.

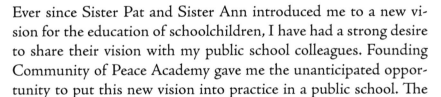

Ever since Sister Pat and Sister Ann introduced me to a new vision for the education of schoolchildren, I have had a strong desire to share their vision with my public school colleagues. Founding Community of Peace Academy gave me the unanticipated opportunity to put this new vision into practice in a public school. The results of this have far exceeded my hopes and dreams.

When our desired outcome is to educate the whole person— mind, body and will—for peace, justice, freedom, compassion, wholeness and fullness of life for all; the world around us shifts. We find ourselves standing on holy ground.

If asked to write their own personal philosophies of education, if asked to express their most dearly held beliefs regarding their work in public education, if asked to state their desired outcome for their own students or for all students attending the public schools of America, what would teachers, parents, union members, board members, members of state and federal governments, researchers, businesspeople, and people on the street tell us? There is no doubt that most would want each public school student to reach his or her full potential and to become a productive and contributing citizen. Our country is filled with good people who want only the best for our children.

Good people work in public schools, and on behalf of public schools, all across the United States. Daily they pour themselves out in service to our nation's children. Their dedication and commitment are legendary. Yet, in spite of their best efforts, in spite of heroic successes in classrooms all across America, too many of these good people do not see their hopes and dreams for their students fulfilled. Heroic outcomes within individual classrooms, within dysfunctional schools, will not change the face of public education in America. We must embrace a vision capable of transforming entire school communities, so as to ensure heroic outcomes for all of the children and youth in America's K–12 schools. There are no easy answers, but there are answers.

As a nation, we are willing to pay billions upon billions of dollars to ensure that every public school student will reach proficiency on state tests by the year 2013. What price are we as a nation willing to pay for wholeness and fullness of life for all of the children and youth who attend our public schools? Achieving such an outcome will exact a very different price. We must lay down the mantle of power and take up the mantle of love.

Where wholeness and fullness of life *for all* is the desired outcome, power has no place. Healthy public schools require servant-leadership at all levels. This new vision will require setting aside practices that divide the public school community into categories of "us and them." Bureaucracy and union influence work against the broad implementation of this new vision. It is possible to put systems in place that promote cooperation, teamwork, and trust. The governance structure of Community of Peace Academy, as described in Chapter 9, is an example of this.

In forty of our fifty states, charter school legislation provides new autonomy to the public school community, thus offering the possibility of creating a more hopeful future for public education. If the next ten thousand charter schools were to wholeheartedly embrace this new vision, we would be well on our way to transforming public education in America.

Creating the conditions for wholeness and fullness of life for all happens first within the human heart. The transformation of our public schools will be accomplished one person at a time. It is those people whose hearts have been transformed by love, who bring peace, hope, joy, and love to every public school in America. We all know and can name such people. They are the ones we will always remember, because they changed our lives for the better.

Creating schools in which the lives of all members of the community may be transformed by love unleashes the innovative energy and passion of every person. The potential for good within such schools is awe-inspiring. Such an outcome is possible within every public school.

Placing blame will not accomplish this. If our nation's public schools are to be transformed in our lifetime, they will be transformed by the highest form of love, which is forgiveness. This new vision transcends our political, social, racial, cultural, and religious differences. We must reach across all such barriers for the sake of our children. Our work will be immeasurably enriched, and our own lives will be transformed in the process.

Many of us who work on behalf of public education are idealists and perfectionists. We want a perfect world and the sooner the better. We feel a tremendous responsibility for the right outcome for our students. We are aware of the ticking clock and the awesome responsibility that we carry on our shoulders. Setting aside our power and control is a difficult thing to do, but we must do it.

Faith in a higher power makes it possible to let go of the need for power and control. Faith in a beneficent higher power frees one from fear and provides the moral courage required to risk transformative change. Most of our nation's great leaders were profoundly aware of this truth.

The public school landscape has never been more challenging, nor has it ever been more hopeful. The future is in the hands of all of us who are passionate about public education. May we courageously reach across the barriers that divide us and humbly join hands in a spirit of forgiveness and hope, bringing to life a new vision for America's public schools; a vision of wholeness and fullness of life for all.

Community of Peace Academy:
Peace and Ethics Curriculum Sources

Growing Communities for Peace: This is a conflict prevention curriculum for primary grades. It incorporates the use of peace circles, peace tables, and conflict resolution steps. The program offers the use of puppets, games, music, and stories.

> Rebecca Janke, M.Ed.
> Education Director
> Growing Communities for Peace
> P.O. Box 281
> Lakeland, MN 55043
> Phone: 651-214-8282
> E-mail: peace@umn.edu

PeaceBuilders: PeaceBuilders is a conflict prevention program appropriate for grades K–8. The program is research based and teaches six basic principles for conflict prevention. It has become the center of our K–8 peace program.

> PeaceBuilders
> PeacePartners, Inc.
> 236 East 3rd Street, Suite 217
> Long Beach, CA 90802-3174
> Phone (toll-free): 877-473-2236
> Web site: www.peacebuilders.com

Heartwood: The Heartwood Program teaches seven ethical principles through the use of multicultural children's literature from around the world.

> The Heartwood Institute
> 425 North Craig Street, Suite 302
> Pittsburgh, PA 15213
> Phone: 800-432-7810
> Web site: www.heartwoodethics.org
> E-mail: hrtwood@heartwoodethics.org

Responsive Classroom: Responsive Classroom requires extensive staff training. It teaches children to be genuinely caring individuals, responsible for their own decisions and actions. Our entire staff is trained in the use of these methods.

> Responsive Classroom
> Origins
> 3805 Grand Avenue South
> Minneapolis, MN 55409
> Phone: 612-822-3422

Project Wisdom: The objectives of this grade 7–12 program are:

+ To encourage students to take responsibility for their choices and actions.
+ To place role models before students by quoting individuals who have contributed to humanity.
+ To teach tolerance and understanding of different races, cultures, and religions.
+ To encourage students to think by asking them questions that require reflection and inner searching.
+ To counteract the negativity in the world with positive thoughts and ideas.

> Project Wisdom
> P.O. Box 270121   4747 Bellaire Boulevard,
> Houston, TX 77277-0121   Suite 210
> Phone: 800-884-4974   Bellaire, TX 77401-4518
> Web site: www.projectwisdom.com
> E-mail: pwteam@projectwisdom.com

Bibliography

Adler, M. J. (1985). *Ten Philosophical Mistakes.* New York: Macmillan.

Anderson, C. S. (1982). The Search for School Climate: A Review of the Literature. *Review of Educational Research*, 52, 368–420.

Anderson, G. L., Herr, K., and Nihlen, A. S. (1994). *Studying Your Own School: An Educator's Guide to Qualitative Practitioner Research.* Thousand Oaks, CA: Corwin Press.

Anson, A. R. (1994). *Risk and Protection during the Middle School Transition: The Role of School Climate in Early Adolescent Development.* (Doctoral dissertation, Northwestern University, 1994). Dissertation Abstracts International, 9521646.

Apple, M. W. (1990). *Ideology and Curriculum*, 2nd ed. New York: Routledge.

Aristotle. (1925). *The Nicomachean Ethics* (Trans. David Ross). New York: Oxford University Press.

Armon, C. (1988). The Place of the Good in a Justice Reasoning Approach to Moral Education. *Journal of Moral Development*, 17 (3), 220–29.

Ayers, W. C., and Miller, J. L. (1998). *A Light in Dark Times: Maxine Greene and the Unfinished Conversation.* New York: Teachers College Press.

Bennett, W. J. (1995). *The Moral Compass: Stories for Life's Journey.* New York: Simon and Schuster.

Benson, P. L., Galbraith, J., and Espland, P. (1995). *What Kids Need to Succeed.* Minneapolis: Free Spirit Publishing.

Benson, P. L., Yeager, R. J., Wood, P. K., Guerra, M. J., and Manno, B. V. (1986). *Catholic High Schools: Their Impact on Low-income Students.* Washington, DC: National Catholic Education Association.

Berman, S. H. (1993). *The Development of Social Responsibility.* (Doctoral dissertation, Harvard University, 1993). Dissertation Abstracts International, 9326300.

Bernardo, R. S. (1997). In Pursuit of the Moral School. *Social Studies Review: Journal of the California Council for the Social Studies*, 37 (1), 43–47.

Bhindi, N., and Duignan, P. (1997). Leadership for a New Century: Authenticity, Intentionality, Spirituality and Sensibility. *Educational Management and Administration*, 25 (2), 117–32

Bogdan, R. C., and Biklen, S. K. (1992). *Qualitative Research for Education.* Needham Heights, MA: Allyn and Bacon.

Bolman, L. G., and Deal, T. E. (1995). *Leading with Soul: An Uncommon Journey of Spirit.* San Francisco: Jossey-Bass.

Bryk, A. S., and Driscoll, M. E. (1988). *The High School as Community: Contextual Influences and Consequences for Students and Teachers.* Madison: University of Wisconsin, Wisconsin Center for Educational Research.

Bryk, A. S., and Raudenbush, S. W. (1989). Toward a More Appropriate Conceptualization of Research on School Effects: A Three-Level Hierarchical Model. In R. D. Bock (Ed.), *Multilevel Analysis of Educational Data.* New York: Academic Press.

Bryk, A. S., and Thum, Y. M. (1989). The Effect of High School Organization upon Dropping Out: An Exploratory Investigation. *American Educational Research Journal*, 26, 353–83.

Buber, M. (1970). *I and Thou* (Trans. W. Kaufmann). New York: Charles Scribner's Sons. (Original work published 1923.)

Capra, F., and Steindl-Rast, D. (1992). *Belonging to the Universe.* New York: HarperCollins.

Cardi, J. J. (1984). *Caring and Community: A Study of Professional Norms and Controls in School.* (Doctoral dissertation, Syracuse University, 1984). Dissertation Abstracts International, 8508213.

Character Education Partnership. (2003). *Becoming a School of Character: Practices to Adopt and Adapt. A How-To Guide.* Washington, DC: Author.

Charney, R. S. (1993). *Teaching Children to Care.* Greenfield, MA: Northeast Foundation for Children.

Charney, R. S. (1997). *Habits of Goodness: Case Studies in the Social Curriculum.* Greenfield, MA: Northeast Foundation for Children.

Chavkin, N. F. (1993). *Families and Schools in a Pluralistic Society.* Albany: State University of New York Press.

Clouse, B. (1983). Church and State in Kohlberg's Approach to Moral Education in Public Schools. *Contemporary Education*, 54 (3), 184–89.

Coleman, J. S. (1985). Schools and the Communities They Serve. *Phi Delta Kappan*, 66, 527–32.

Coleman, J. S. (1988). Social Capital in the Creation of Human Capital. *American Journal of Sociology*, 94 (Suppl.), S95–S120.

Coleman, J. S., and Hoffer, T. (1987). *Public and Private High Schools: The Impact of Communities*. New York: Basic Books.

Coleman, J. S., Hoffer, T., and Kilgore, S. (1982). *High School Achievement: Public, Catholic, and Private Schools Compared*. New York: Basic Books.

Coleman, M. D. (1993). *Teacher Perceptions of a Caring Middle School*. (Doctoral dissertation, Columbia University Teachers College, 1993). Dissertation Abstracts International, 9414423.

Coles, R. (1997). *The Moral Intelligence of Children: How to Raise a Moral Child*. New York: Plume Books.

Convey, J. J. (1992). *Catholic Schools Make A Difference: Twenty-five Years of Research*. Washington, DC: National Catholic Education Association.

Covaleskie, J. F. (1992). Discipline and Morality: Beyond Rules and Consequences. *Educational Forum*, 56 (no. 2), 173–83.

Cummins, J. (1986). Empowering Minority Students: A Framework for Intervention. *Harvard Educational Review*, 56 (no. 1), 10–36.

Curwin, R. L., and Mendler, A. N. (1988). *Discipline with Dignity*. Alexandria, VA: Association for Supervision and Curriculum Development.

Daniels, H., Bizar, M., and Zemelman, S. (2001). *Rethinking High School*. Portsmouth, NH: Heinemann.

Daniels, H., and Zemelman, S. (2004). *Subjects Matter: Every Teacher's Guide to Content-Area Teaching*. Portsmouth, NH: Heinemann

Danielson, C. (1996). *Enhancing Professional Practice: A Framework for Teaching*. Alexandria, VA: Association for Supervision and Curriculum Development.

Deal, T. E., and Peterson, K. D. (1999). *Shaping School Culture: The Heart of Leadership*. San Francisco: Jossey-Bass.

Eccles, J. S., Wigfield, A., Midgley, C., Reuman, D., MacIver, D., and Feldlaufer, H. (1993). Negative Effects of Traditional Middle Schools on Students' Motivation. *Elementary School Journal*, 93, 553–74.

Echevarria, J., Vogt, M., and Short, D. J. (2000). *Making Content Comprehensible to English Language Learners: The SIOP Model.* Needham Heights, MA: Allyn & Bacon.

EdVisions. (2006). Hope Study. Ron Newell, EdVisions (Ron@EdVisions.coop) or Mark J. Van Ryzin, University of Minnesota (Vanr0040@umn.edu).

Edwards, V. B. (1999). Demanding Results. *Education Week,* 18 (17), 5.

Elkind, D. (1994). School and Family in the Postmodern World. *Phi Delta Kappa,* 77 (1), 8–14.

Etzioni, A. (1993). *The Spirit of Community: The Reinventing of American Society.* New York: Touchstone.

Foucault, M. (1980). *Power/Knowledge: Selected Interviews and Writings, 1972–1977* (Trans. C. Gordon, L. Marshall, J. Mepham, K. Soper). New York: Pantheon.

Foucault, M. (1995). *Discipline and Punish: The Birth of the Prison,* 2nd ed. (Trans. A. Sheridan). New York: Vintage Books. (Original work published 1975.)

Forcey, L. R., and Harris, I. M. (1999). *Peacebuilding for Adolescents: Strategies for Educators and Community Leaders.* New York: Peter Lang.

Freire, P. (1996). *Pedagogy of the Oppressed* (new rev. 20th-anniversary ed.) (Trans. M. B. Ramos). New York: Continuum. (Original work published 1970.)

Goodlad, J. I., Soder, R., and Sirotnik, K. A. (1990). *The Moral Dimensions of Teaching.* San Francisco: Jossey-Bass.

Gorman, M. J. (1991). *Crossroads: Integrated Models for Teaching Ethics and Spirituality.* ERIC Digest, ED349243.

Grant, G. (1981). The Character of Education and the Education of Character. *Daedalus,* 110, 135–49.

Grant G. (1985). Schools That Make an Impact: Creating a Strong Ethos. In J. H. Bunzel (Ed.), *Challenge to American Schools: The Case for Standards and Values.* New York: Oxford University Press.

Grant, G. (1988). *The World We Created at Hamilton High.* Cambridge, MA: Harvard University Press.

Greeley, A. M. (1982). *Catholic High Schools and Minority Students.* New Brunswick, NJ: Transaction Books.

Greeley, A. M. (1989). My Research on Catholic Schools. *Chicago Studies,* 28, 245–63.

Groome, T. H. (1991). *Sharing Faith: A Comprehensive Approach to Religious Education and Pastoral Ministry.* San Francisco: HarperSanFrancisco.

Groome, T. (1998). *Educating for Life: A Spiritual Vision for Every Teacher and Parent.* Allen, TX: Thomas More.

Hannaway, J., and Abramowitz, S. (1985). Public and Private Schools: Are They Really Different? In G. R. Austin and H. Garber (Eds.), *Research on Exemplary Schools.* New York: Academic Press.

Heath, D. H. (1994). *Schools of Hope: Developing Mind and Character in Today's Youth.* San Francisco: Jossey-Bass.

Huffman, H. A. (1994). *Developing a Character Education Program: One School's Experience.* Alexandria, VA: Association for Supervision and Curriculum Development.

Jennings, K., Stahl-Wert, J., and Blanchard Family Partnership. (2003). *The Serving Leader.* San Francisco: Berrett-Koehler.

Kant, I. (1995). *Foundations of the Metaphysics of Morals,* 2nd ed. (Trans. L. W. Beck). Upper Saddle River, NJ: Prentice Hall (Original work published 1785.)

Kohlberg, L. (1966). Moral Education in the Schools: A Developmental View. *School Review,* 74 (1), 1–30.

Kohn, A. (1986). *No Contest: The Case against Competition.* Boston: Houghton Mifflin.

Kolderie, T., Graba, J., and Schroeder, J. (2005). *Education Finance. More Money or Different Spending Choices: What Factors Make a Difference?* St. Paul, MN: education/evolving.

Kozol, J. (2000). *Ordinary Resurrections: Children in the Years of Hope.* New York: Crown.

Kratzer, C. C. (1996). *Redefining Effectiveness: Cultivating a Caring Community in an Urban Elementary School.* (Doctoral dissertation, University of California, 1996). Dissertation Abstracts International, 9632847.

Kunjufu, J. (1986). *Countering the Conspiracy to Destroy Black Boys,* vol. 2. Chicago: African American Images.

Landsman, J. (1993). *Basic Needs: A Year with Street Kids in City Schools.* Minneapolis: Milkweed Editions.

Lee, P. K. (1993). *A Case Study: Students' Perceptions of Caring Manners of Educational Leaders and Its Relation to Their Learning Outcomes.* (Doctoral dissertation, Florida State University, 1993). Dissertation Abstracts International, 9317644.

Lee, V. E., and Bryk, A. S. (1988). Curriculum Tracking as Mediating the Social Distribution of High School Achievement. *Sociology and Education*, 61, 78–94.

Lee, V. E., and Bryk, A. S. (1989). A Multilevel Model of the Social Distribution of High School Achievement. *Sociology of Education*, 62, 172–79.

Lee, V. E., and Stewart, C. (1989). *National Assessment of Educational Progress Proficiency in Mathematics and Science, 1985–1986: Catholic and Public Schools Compared*. Washington, DC: National Catholic Education Association.

Lickona, T. (1991). *Educating for Character: How Our Schools Can Teach Respect and Responsibility*. New York: Bantam Books.

Lightfoot, S. L. (1983). *The Good High School: Portraits of Character and Culture*. New York: Basic Books:

Lipsitz, J. (1984). *Successful Schools for Young Adolescents*. New Brunswick, NJ: Transaction Books.

Marks, H. M., and Lee, V. E. (1989). *National Assessment of Educational Progress Proficiency in Reading, 1985–1986: Catholic and Public Schools Compared*. Washington, DC: National Catholic Education Association.

Marshall, C., and Rossman, G. B. (1995). *Designing Qualitative Research*, 2nd ed. Thousand Oaks, CA: Sage.

McCreery, E. (1994). *Towards an Understanding of the Notion of the Spiritual in Education*. ERIC Digest, EJ488487.

Meier, D. (1995). *The Power of Their Ideas: Lessons for America from a Small School in Harlem*. Boston: Beacon Press.

Miller, R. (Ed.). (1991). *New Directions in Education: Selections from Holistic Education Review*. ERIC Digest, ED406460.

Minnesota Department of Health. (2003). *Adolescent Health among Minnesota's Racial/Ethnic Groups: Progress and Disparities*. St. Paul: Author.

Minnesota Department of Health. (2004, Spring). *Population Health Assessment Quarterly. Vol. 4, no. 2: Suicidal Thoughts and Attempts among Minnesota Teens*. St. Paul: Author.

Moffet, J. (1994). *The Universal School House: Spiritual Awakening through Education*. San Francisco: Jossey-Bass.

Moore, T. (1991). *Care of the Soul: A Guide for Cultivating Depth and Sacredness in Everyday Life*. New York: HarperCollins.

Muuss, R. E. (1976). Kohlberg's Cognitive-Developmental Approach to Adolescent Morality. *Adolescence*, 11 (41), 39–58.

Niebuhr, R. (1952). *The Irony of American History: The Position of America in the World Community in Light of Her History*. New York: Charles Scribner's Sons.

Noddings, N. (1992). *The Challenge to Care in Schools*. New York: Teachers College Press.

Noddings, N. (2002). *Educating Moral People: A Caring Alternative to Character Education*. New York: Teachers College Press.

O'Hare, P. (1983). *Education for Peace and Justice*. New York: Harper and Row.

Olson, L., and Jerald, C. D. (1998). Barriers to Success. *Education Week*, 17 (17), 9–13.

Palmer, P. (1993). *To Know as We Are Known: Education as a Spiritual Journey*. San Francisco: Harper.

Palmer, P. (1998). *The Courage to Teach: Exploring the Inner Landscape of a Teacher's Life*. San Francisco: Jossey-Bass.

Palmer, Parker. (1999). *Let Your Life Speak: Listening for the Voice of Vocation*. San Francisco: Jossey-Bass.

Palmer, Parker (2004). *A Hidden Wholeness: The Journey toward an Undivided Life*. San Franciso: Josey-Bass.

Parks Daloz, L. A., Keen, C. H., Keen, J. P., and Daloz Parks, S. (1996). *Common Fire: Leading Lives of Commitment in a Complex World*. Boston: Beacon Press.

Purkey, S. C., and Smith, M. S. (1985). Educational Policy and School Effectiveness. In G. R. Austin and H. Garber (Eds.), *Research on Exemplary Schools*. New York: Academic Press.

Rogers, C. R. (1961). *On Becoming a Person: A Therapist's View of Psychotherapy*. Boston: Houghton Mifflin.

Rose, M. (1989). *Lives on the Boundary*. New York: Penguin Books.

Rutter, M., Maughan, B., Morimore, P., Ouston, J., and Smith, A. (1979). *Fifteen Thousand Hours: Secondary Schools and Their Effect on Children*. Cambridge, MA: Harvard University Press.

Schmoker, M. (2006). *Results Now: How We Can Achieve Unprecedented Improvements in Teaching and Learning*. Alexandria, VA: Association for Supervision and Curriculum Development.

Sergiovanni, T. J. (1992). *Moral Leadership: Getting to the Heart of School Improvement.* San Francisco: Jossey-Bass.

Sergiovanni, T. J. (1993). *Building Community in Schools.* San Francisco: Jossey-Bass.

Smyth, J. (1994). *Critical Perspectives on Educational Leadership.* Philadelphia: Falmer Press.

Snyder, C. R., Harris, C., Anderson, J. R., Holleran, S. A., Irving, L. M., Sigmon, S. T., Yoshinobu, L., Gibb, J., Langelle, C., and Harney, P. (1991). The Will and the Ways: Development and Validation of an Individual-Differences Measure of Hope. *Journal of Personality and Social Psychology, 60,* 575–85.

Spindler, G. (1982). *Doing the Ethnography of Schooling.* New York: Holt, Rhinehart and Winston.

Strike, K. (1990). The Legal and Moral Responsibility of Teachers. In J. I. Goodlad, R. Soder, and K. A. Sirotnik (Eds.), *The Moral Dimensions of Teaching.* San Francisco: Jossey-Bass.

Suskind, R. (1998). *A Hope in the Unseen.* New York: Broadway Books.

Takaki, R. (1993). *A Different Mirror.* Boston: Little, Brown.

Taulbert, C. L. (1997). *Eight Habits of the Heart: Embracing Values That Build Strong Families and Communities.* New York: Penguin Books.

Thor, K. A. (1997). *Belonging and Social Support in Educational Settings: A Review and Critique of the Research.* Research report no. 21. Minneapolis: University of Minnesota, College of Education and Human Development.

U.S. Department of Education, Office of Innovation and Improvement. (2004). *Successful Charter Schools.* Contract # ED-01-C0-0012, Task Order D010, with WestEd.

U.S. Department of Education. (2004). *Toward a New Golden Age in American Education: How the Internet, the Law and Today's Students Are Revolutionizing Expectations.* Washington, DC: Author.

Vitullo-Martin, T. (1979). *Catholic Inner City Schools: The Future.* Washington, DC: United States Catholic Conference.

Wingspread Declaration on School Connections. (2004). *Journal of School Health,* 74 (7), 233–34.

Wolf, A. D. (1996). *Nurturing the Spirit in Non-Sectarian Classrooms.* Holidaysburg, PA: Parent Child Press.

To order additional copies of *Success in Education through Peace, Healing, and Hope*

Web:	www.itascabooks.com
Phone:	1-800-901-3480
Fax:	Copy and fill out the form below with credit card information. Fax to 763-398-0198.
Mail:	Copy and fill out the form below. Mail with check or credit card information to:

Syren Book Company
5120 Cedar Lake Road
Minneapolis, MN 55416

Order Form

Copies	Title / Author	Price	Totals
	Success in Education through Peace, Healing, and Hope / Karen J. Rusthoven	$16.95	$
	Subtotal		$
	7% sales tax (MN only)		$
	Shipping and handling, first copy		$ 4.00
	Shipping and handling, ___ add'l copies @$1.00 ea.		$
	TOTAL TO REMIT		$

Payment Information:

__ Check Enclosed __ Visa/MasterCard	
Card number:	Expiration date:
Name on card:	
Billing address:	
City:	State: Zip:
Signature:	Date:

Shipping Information:

__ Same as billing address __ Other (enter below)	
Name:	
Address:	
City:	State: Zip: